A TO Z

This book belongs to

COLOR PAGE!

A

DIRECTIONS: PRACTICE TRACING WRITING EACH LETTER IN THE SPACE PROVIDED.

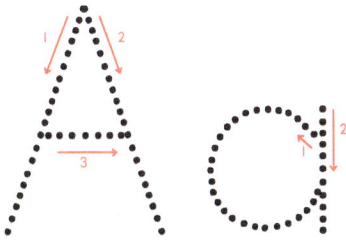

A a

A A A A A A

A A A A A A

A

A

DIRECTIONS: PRACTICE TRACING AND WRITING EACH LETTER IN THE SPACE PROVIDED.

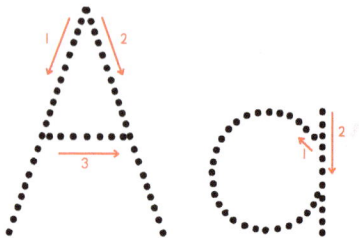

A a

a   a   a   a   a   a

a   a   a   a   a   a

a

a

DIRECTIONS: PRACTICE TRACING AND WRITING EACH LETTER IN THE SPACE PROVIDED.

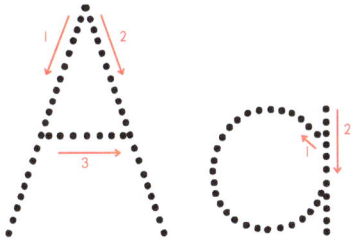

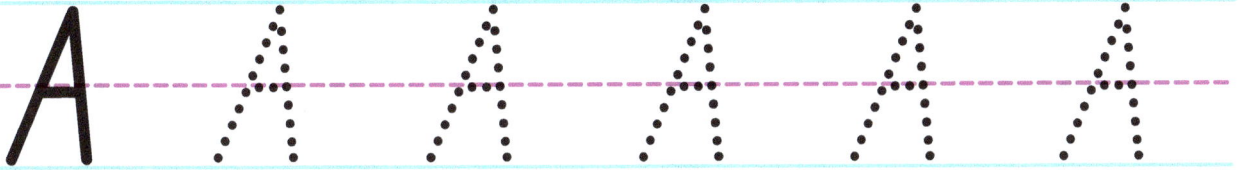

A a

A   A   A   A   A   A

a   a   a   a   a   a

A

a

B

DIRECTIONS: PRACTICE TRACING AND WRITING EACH LETTER IN THE SPACE PROVIDED.

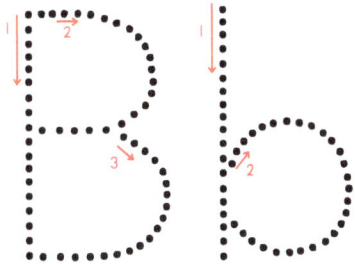

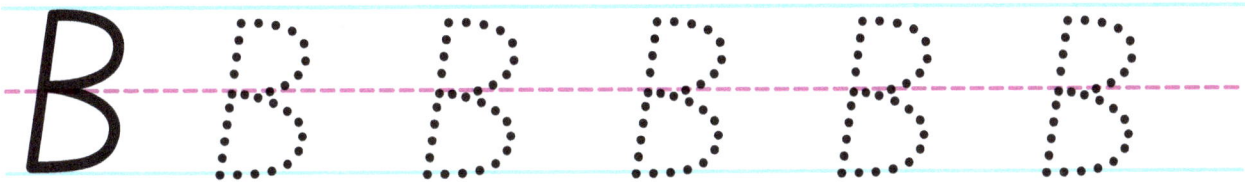

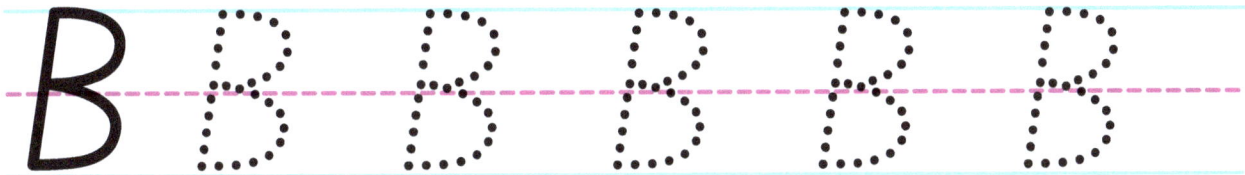

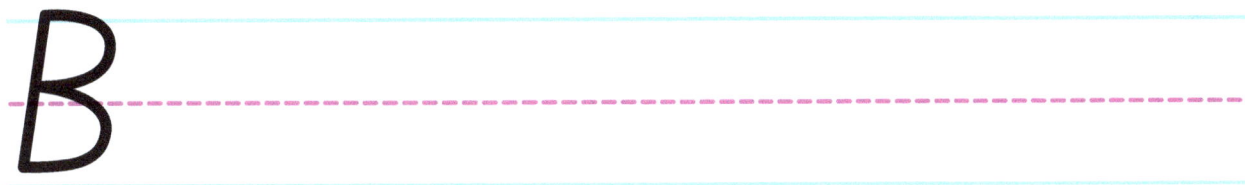

Bb

B B B B B B

B B B B B B

B

B

DIRECTIONS: PRACTICE TRACING AND WRITING EACH LETTER IN THE SPACE PROVIDED.

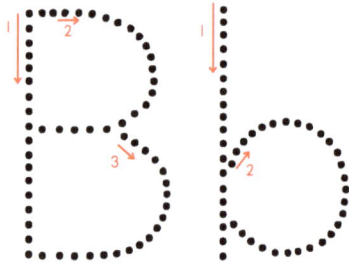

Bb

b   b   b   b   b   b

b   b   b   b   b   b

b

b

DIRECTIONS: PRACTICE TRACING AND WRITING EACH LETTER IN THE SPACE PROVIDED.

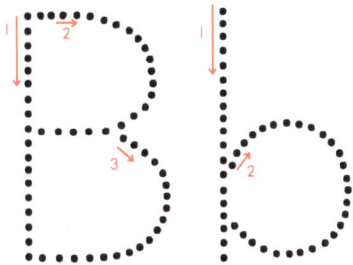

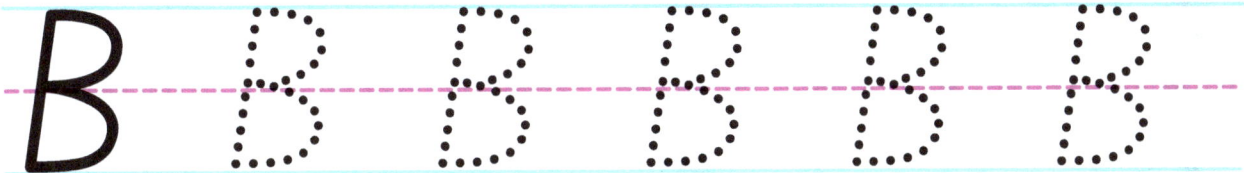

B b

B   B   B   B   B   B

b   b   b   b   b   b

B

b

C

DIRECTIONS: PRACTICE TRACING AND WRITING EACH LETTER IN THE SPACE PROVIDED.

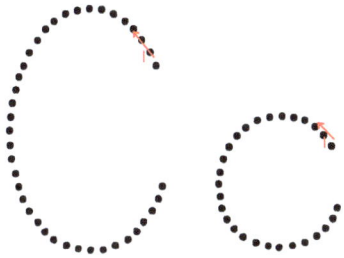

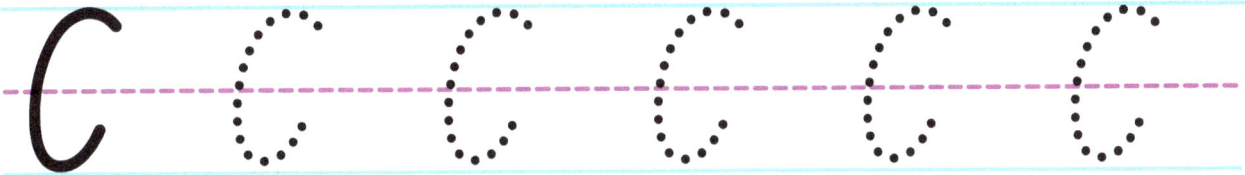

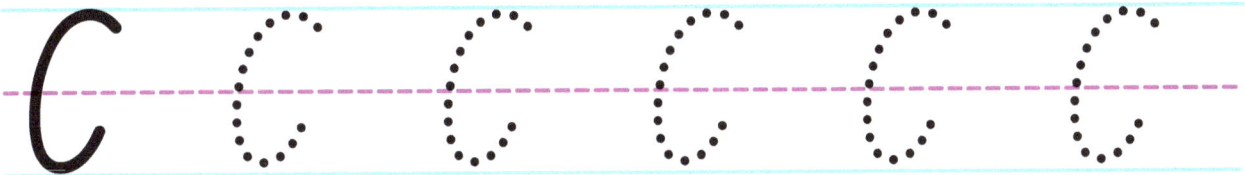

C c

C C C C C C C C C C C

C C C C C C C C C C C

C

C

DIRECTIONS: PRACTICE TRACING AND WRITING EACH LETTER IN THE SPACE PROVIDED.

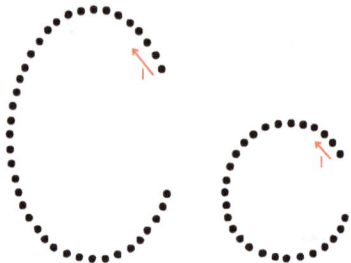

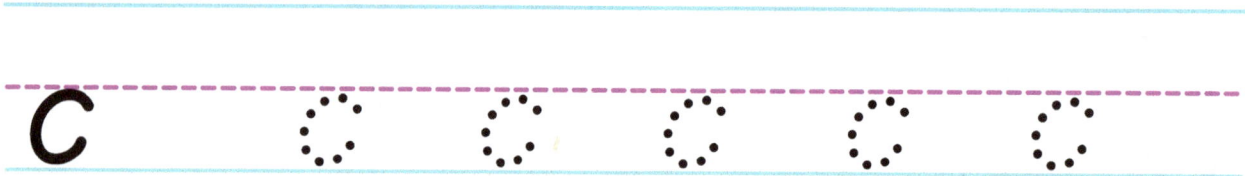

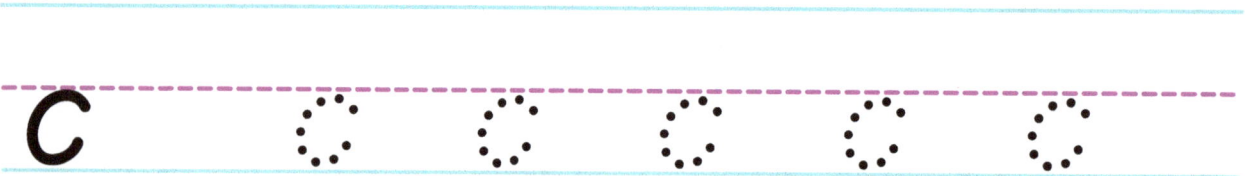

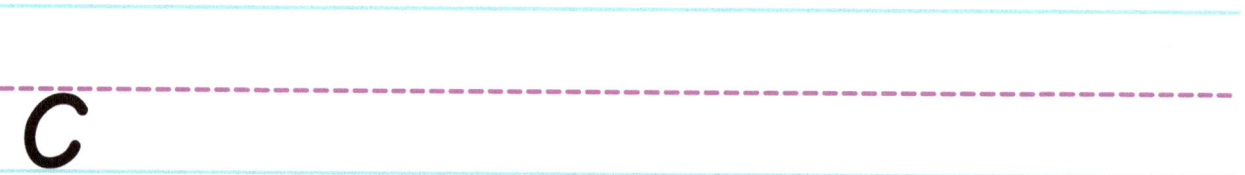

C c

C   c   c   c   c   c

C   c   c   c   c   c

C

C

DIRECTIONS: PRACTICE TRACING AND WRITING EACH LETTER IN THE SPACE PROVIDED.

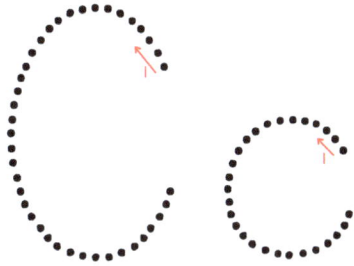

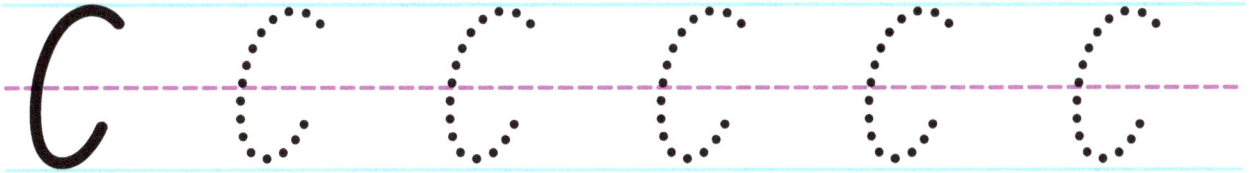

C c

C C C C C C

c c c c c c

C

c

DIRECTIONS: PRACTICE TRACING AND WRITING EACH LETTER IN THE SPACE PROVIDED.

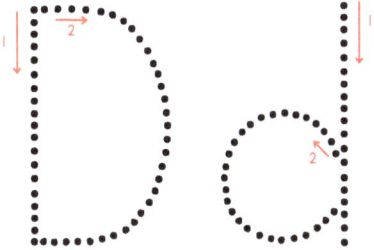

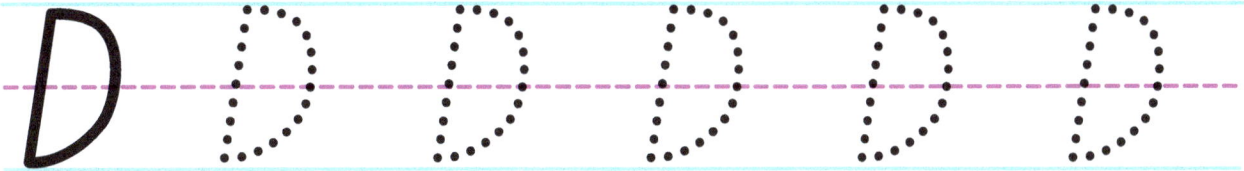

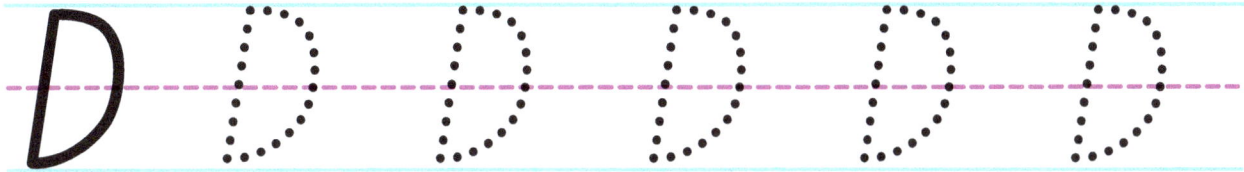

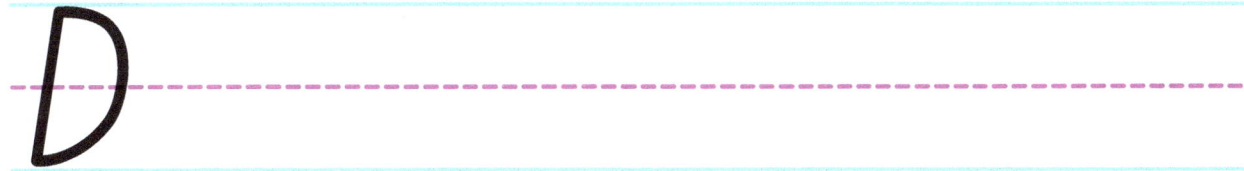

D d

DIRECTIONS: PRACTICE TRACING AND WRITING EACH LETTER IN THE SPACE PROVIDED.

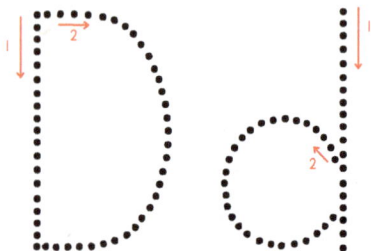

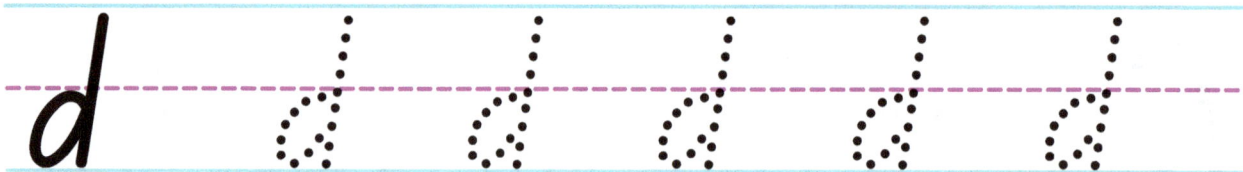

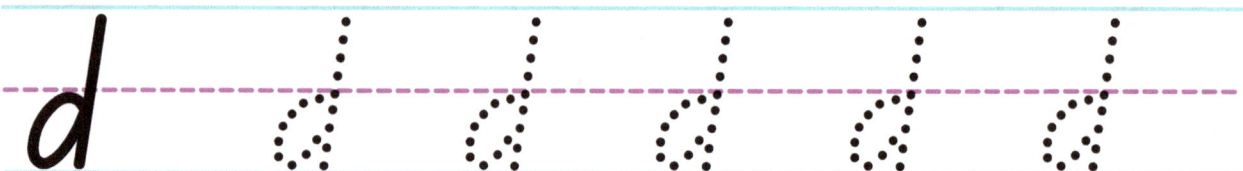

D d

d   d d d d d

d   d d d d d

d

d

DIRECTIONS: PRACTICE TRACING AND WRITING EACH LETTER IN THE SPACE PROVIDED.

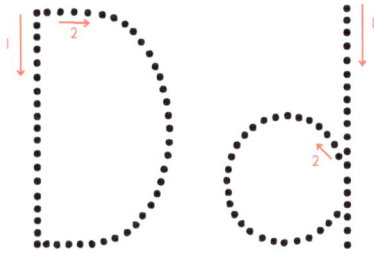

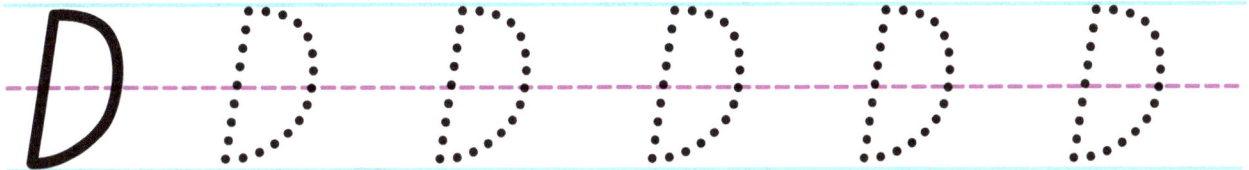

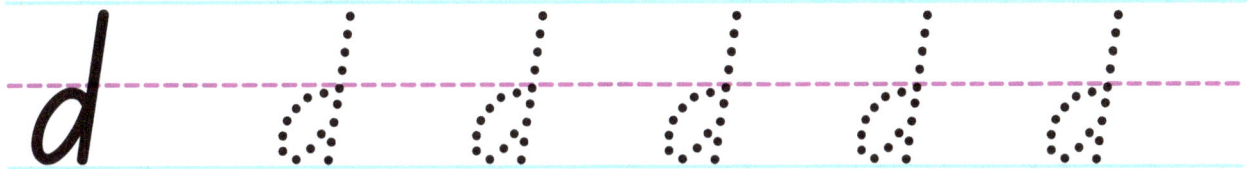

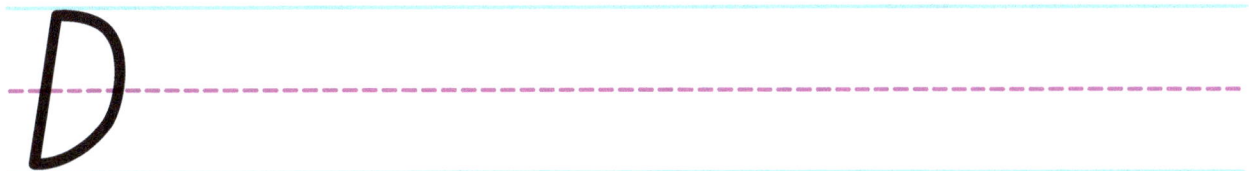

Dd

D D D D D D

d d d d d d

D

d

DIRECTIONS: PRACTICE TRACING AND WRITING EACH LETTER IN THE SPACE PROVIDED.

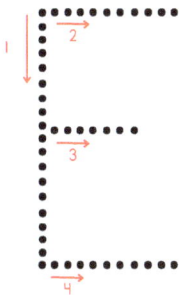

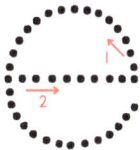

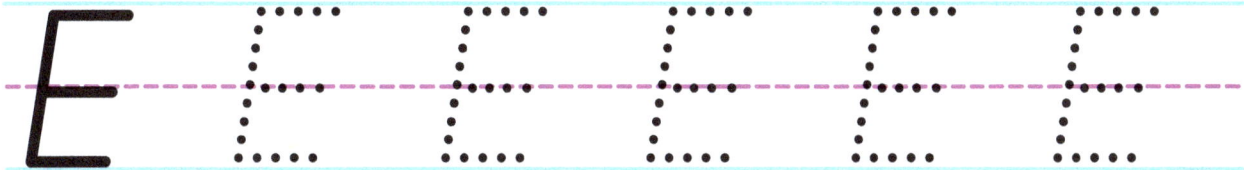

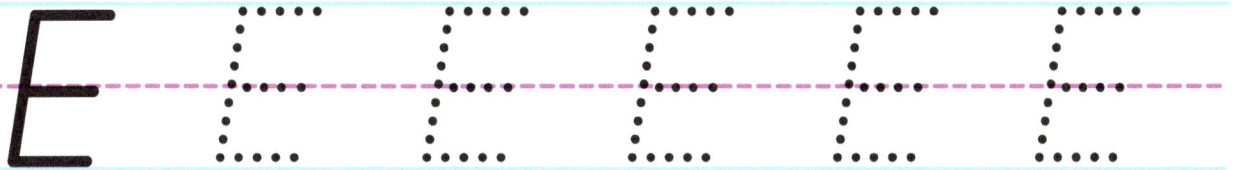

E e

E E E E E E E

E E E E E E E

E

E

DIRECTIONS: PRACTICE TRACING AND WRITING EACH LETTER IN THE SPACE PROVIDED.

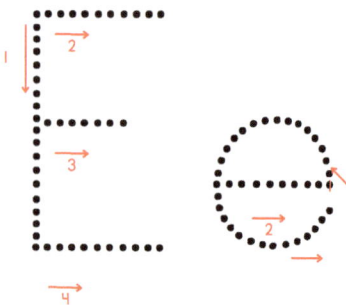

E e

e   e   e   e   e   e

e   e   e   e   e   e

e

e

DIRECTIONS: PRACTICE TRACING AND WRITING EACH LETTER IN THE SPACE PROVIDED.

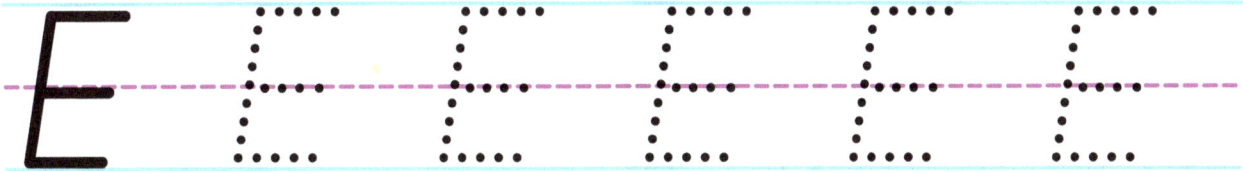

E e

E E E E E E

e e e e e e

E

e e e e e e

DIRECTIONS: PRACTICE TRACING AND WRITING EACH LETTER IN THE SPACE PROVIDED.

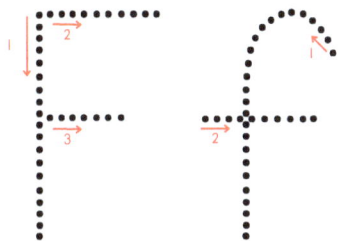

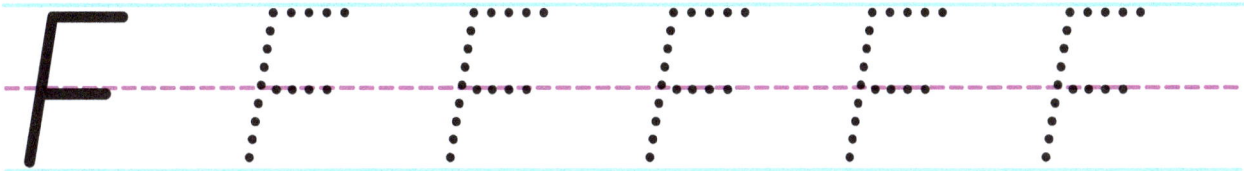

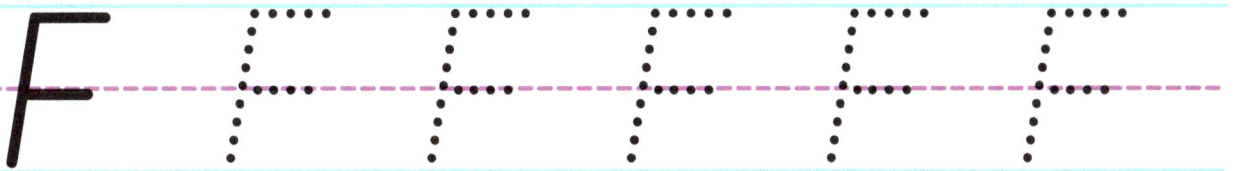

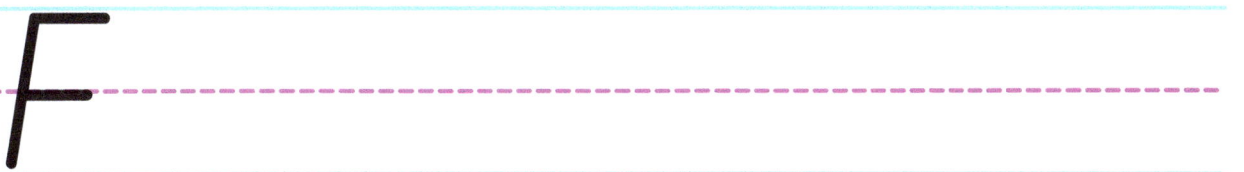

F f

F   F   F   F   F   F

F   F   F   F   F   F

F

F

DIRECTIONS: PRACTICE TRACING AND WRITING EACH LETTER IN THE SPACE PROVIDED.

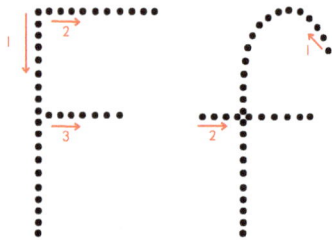

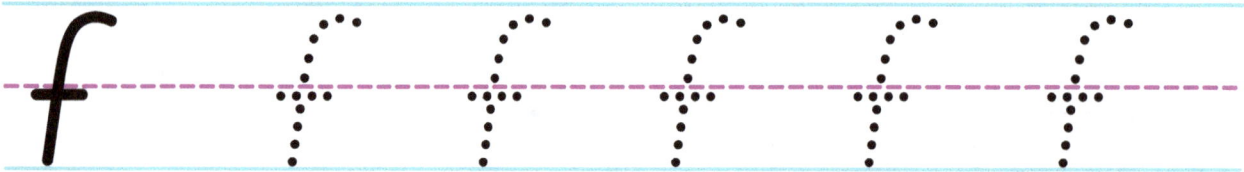

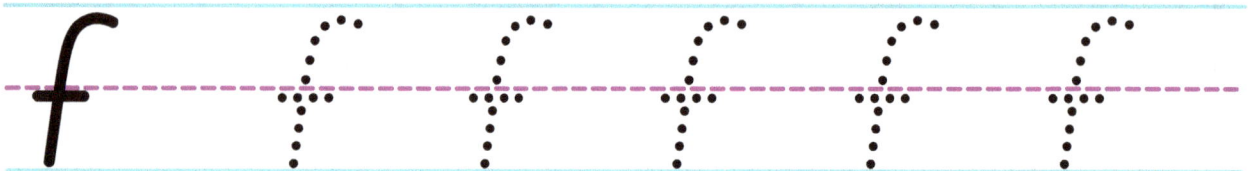

F f

f   f f f f f

f   f f f f f

f

f

DIRECTIONS: PRACTICE TRACING AND WRITING EACH LETTER IN THE SPACE PROVIDED.

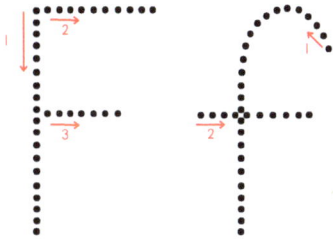

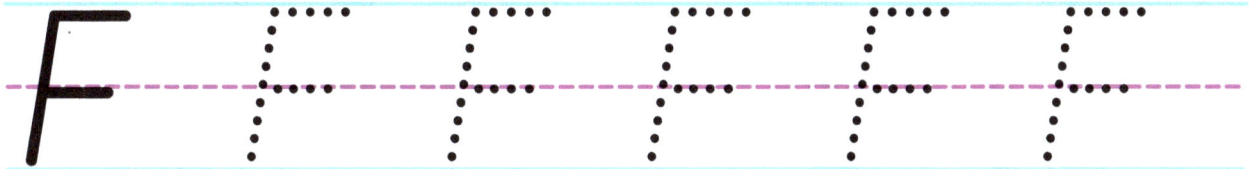

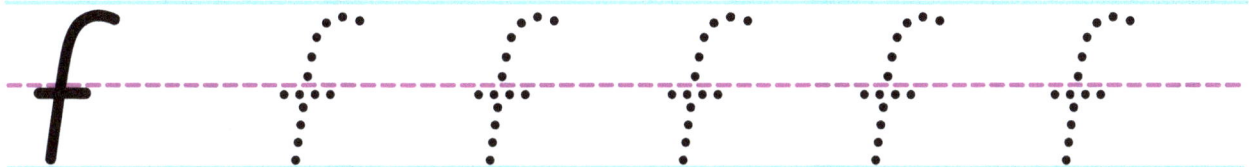

F f

F F F F F F

f f f f f f

F

f

G

DIRECTIONS: PRACTICE TRACING AND WRITING EACH LETTER IN THE SPACE PROVIDED.

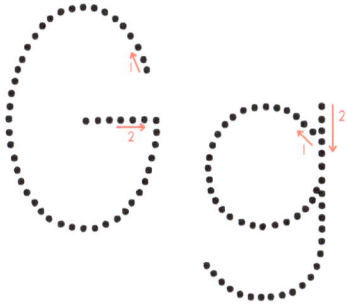

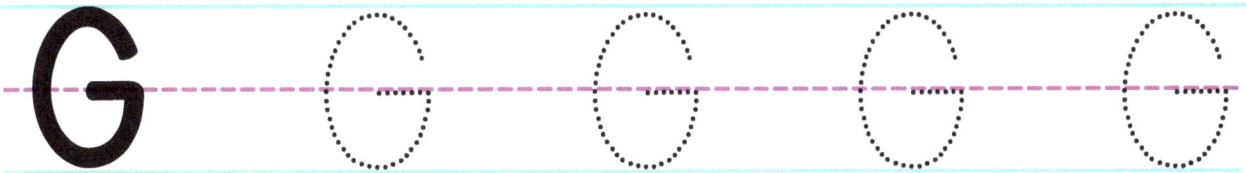

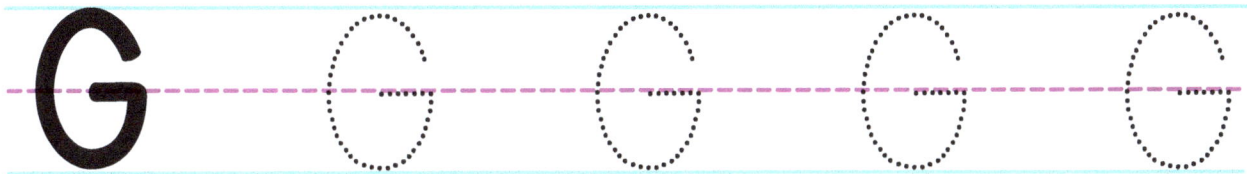

Gg

G G G G G

G G G G G

G G G G G

G G G G G

DIRECTIONS: PRACTICE TRACING AND WRITING EACH LETTER IN THE SPACE PROVIDED.

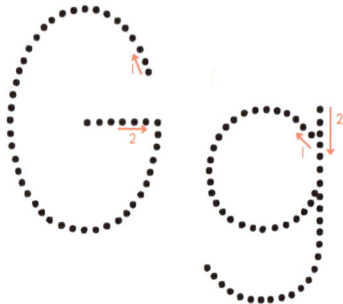

Gg

g g g g g g

g g g g g g

g

g

DIRECTIONS: PRACTICE TRACING AND WRITING EACH LETTER IN THE SPACE PROVIDED.

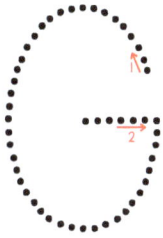

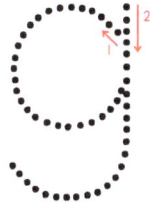

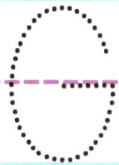

G g

G   G   G   G   G

g   g   g   g   g   g

G   G   G   G   G

g

H

DIRECTIONS: PRACTICE TRACING AND WRITING EACH LETTER IN THE SPACE PROVIDED.

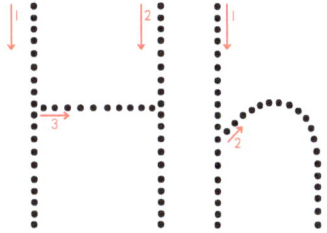

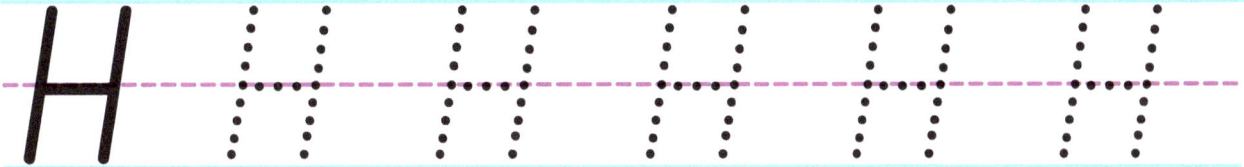

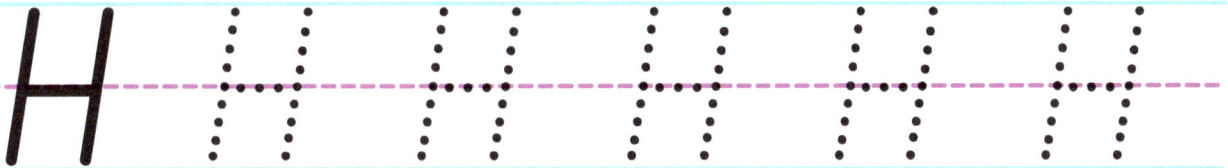

Hh

H H H H H H H

H H H H H H

H

H

DIRECTIONS: PRACTICE TRACING AND WRITING EACH LETTER IN THE SPACE PROVIDED.

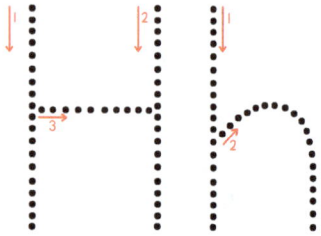

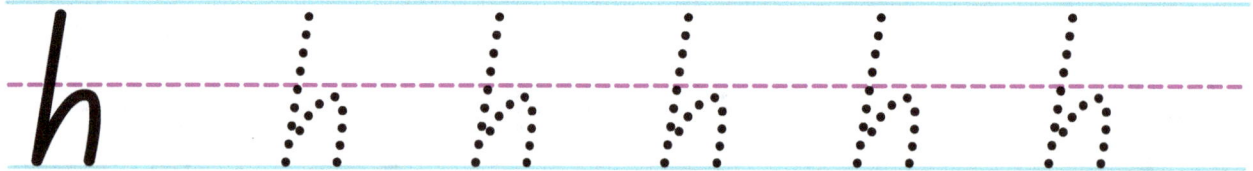

Hh

DIRECTIONS: PRACTICE TRACING AND WRITING EACH LETTER IN THE SPACE PROVIDED.

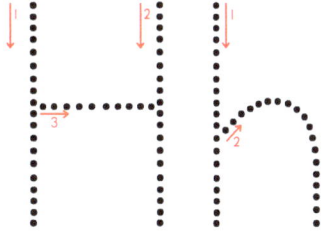

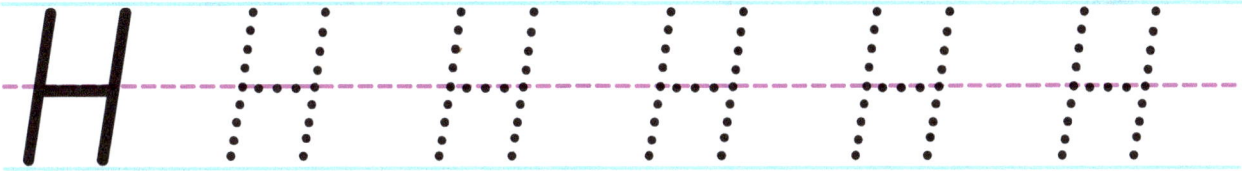

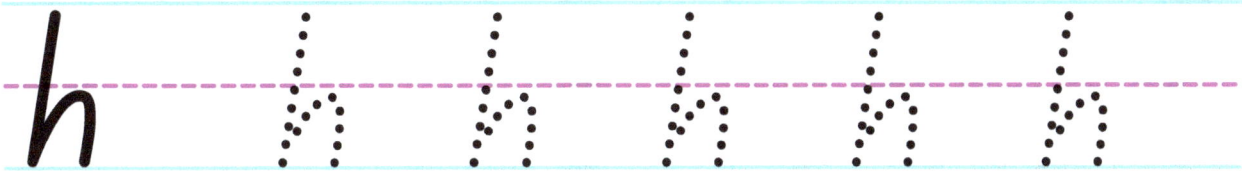

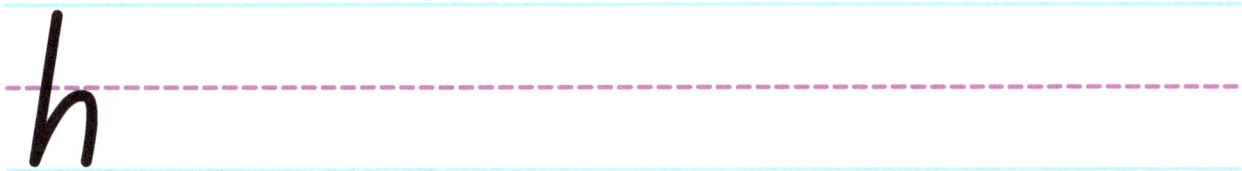

H h

H H H H H H H

h h h h h h

H

h

DIRECTIONS: PRACTICE TRACING AND WRITING EACH LETTER IN THE SPACE PROVIDED.

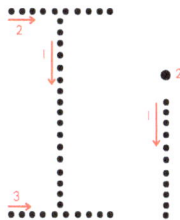

I   i

I   I   I   I   I

I   I   I   I   I

I   I   I   I   I

I   I   I   I   I

DIRECTIONS: PRACTICE TRACING AND WRITING EACH LETTER IN THE SPACE PROVIDED.

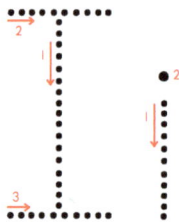

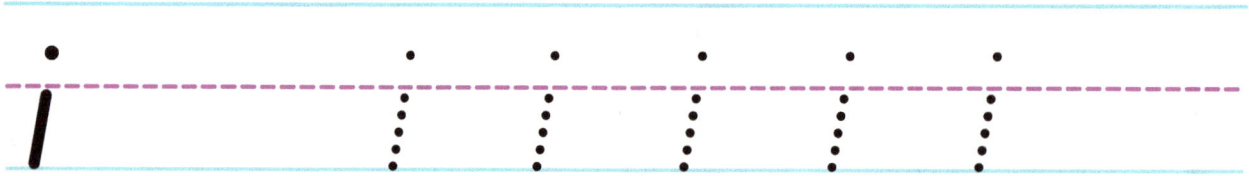

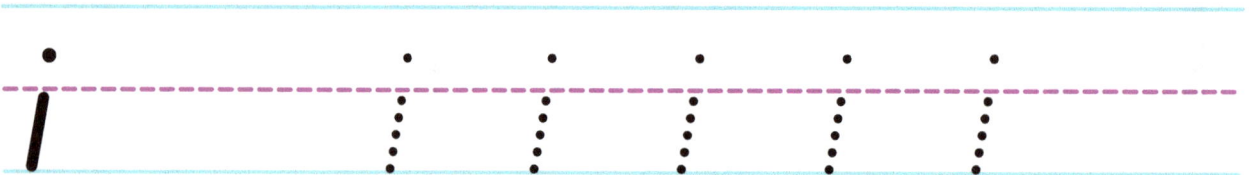

DIRECTIONS: PRACTICE TRACING AND WRITING EACH LETTER IN THE SPACE PROVIDED.

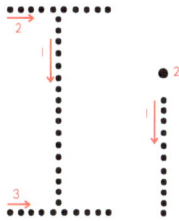

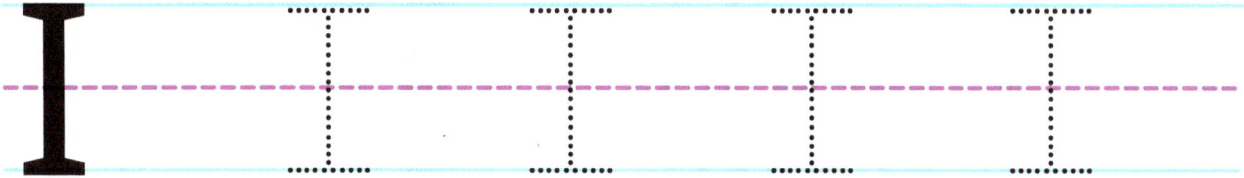

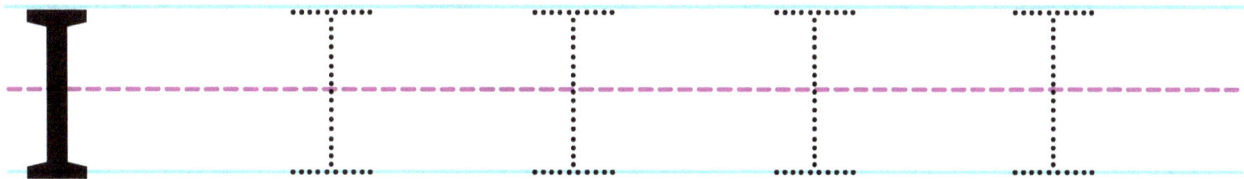

I i

I I I I I

i i i i i i i

I I I I I

i

JAM

DIRECTIONS: PRACTICE TRACING AND WRITING EACH LETTER IN THE SPACE PROVIDED.

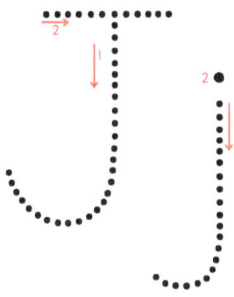

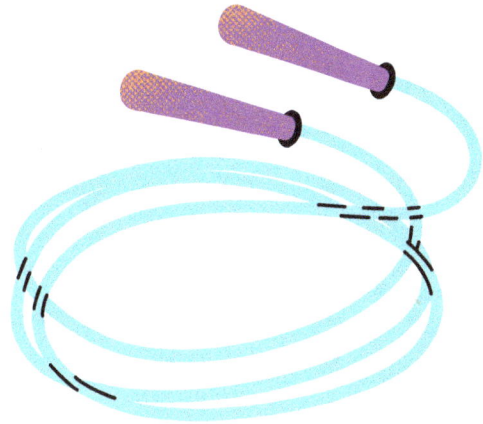

J j

J J J J J

J J J J J

J J J J J

J J J J J

DIRECTIONS: PRACTICE TRACING AND WRITING EACH LETTER IN THE SPACE PROVIDED.

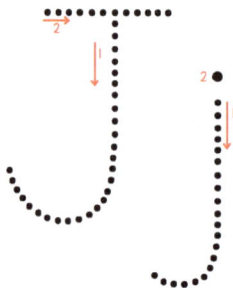

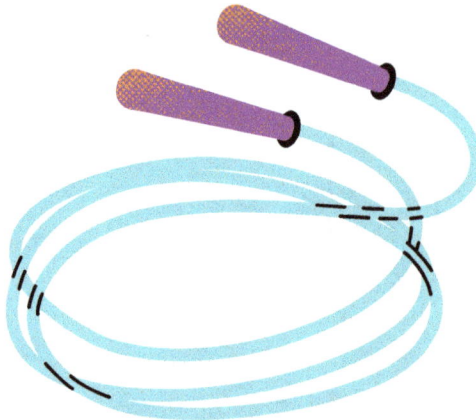

j   J J J J J

j   J J J J J

j

j

DIRECTIONS: PRACTICE TRACING AND WRITING EACH LETTER IN THE SPACE PROVIDED.

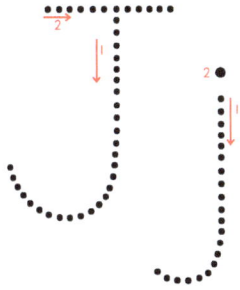

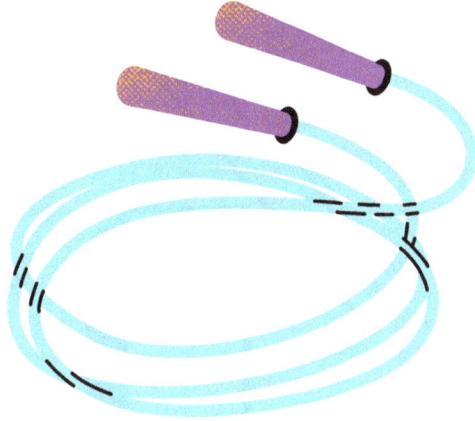

J j

J   J   J   J   J

j   j   j   j   j

J

j

K

DIRECTIONS: PRACTICE TRACING AND WRITING EACH LETTER IN THE SPACE PROVIDED.

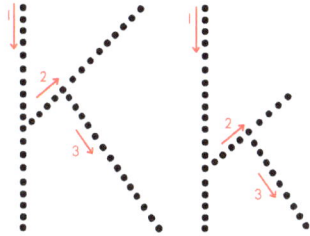

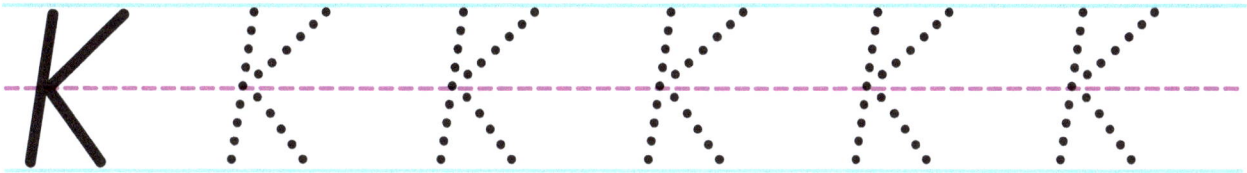

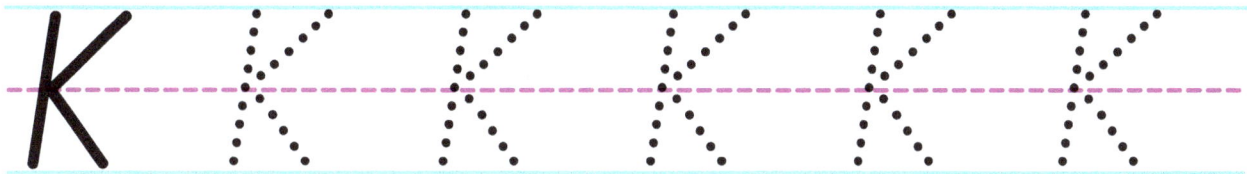

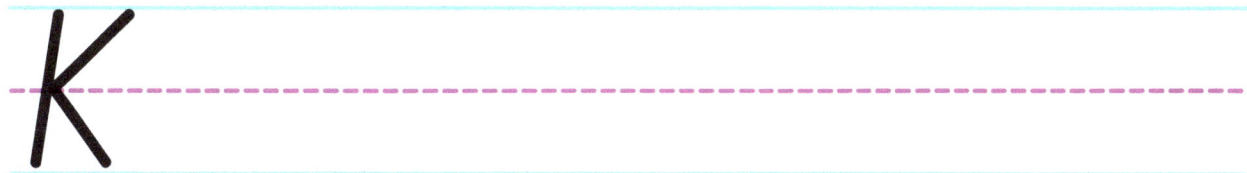

K k

K K K K K K

K K K K K K

K

K

DIRECTIONS: PRACTICE TRACING AND WRITING EACH LETTER IN THE SPACE PROVIDED.

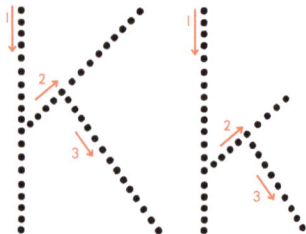

Kk

k k k k k

k k k k k

k

k

DIRECTIONS: PRACTICE TRACING AND WRITING EACH LETTER IN THE SPACE PROVIDED.

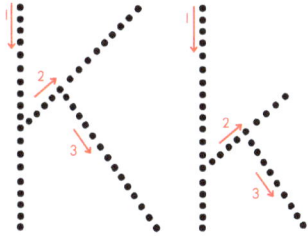

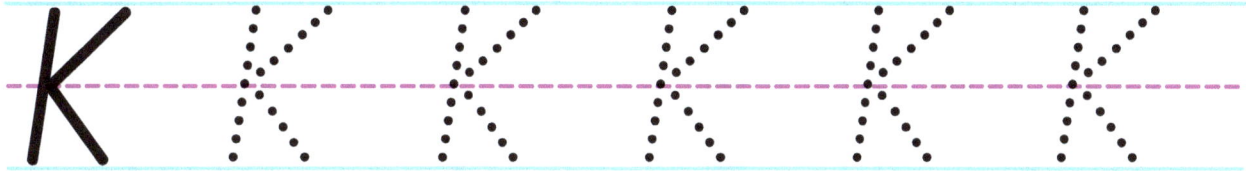

K k

K K K K K K K

k

K

k

DIRECTIONS: PRACTICE TRACING AND WRITING EACH LETTER IN THE SPACE PROVIDED.

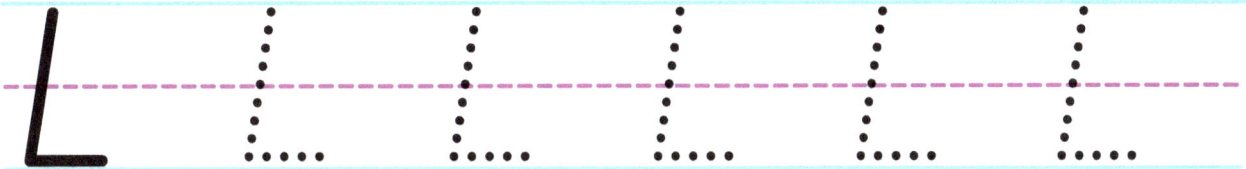

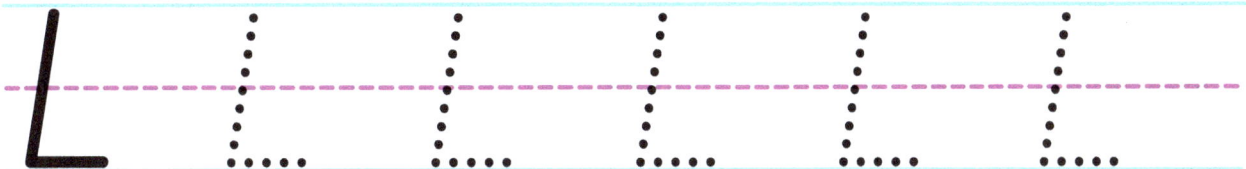

L   L   L   L   L   L

L   L   L   L   L   L

L

L

DIRECTIONS: PRACTICE TRACING AND WRITING EACH LETTER IN THE SPACE PROVIDED.

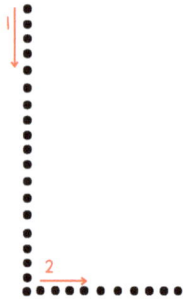

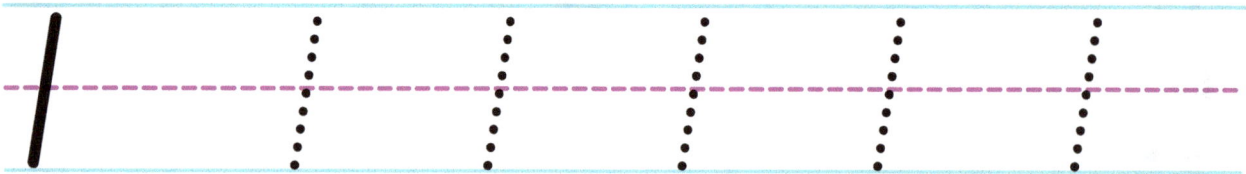

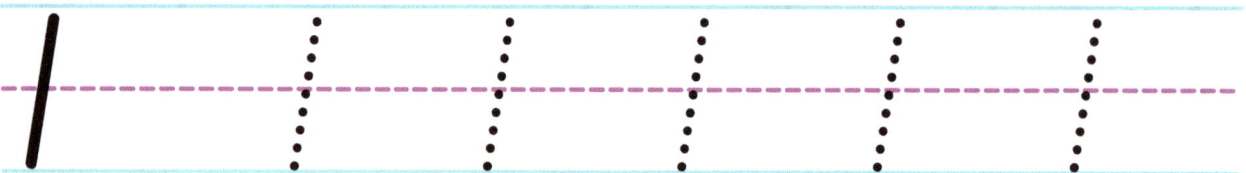

DIRECTIONS: PRACTICE TRACING AND WRITING EACH LETTER IN THE SPACE PROVIDED.

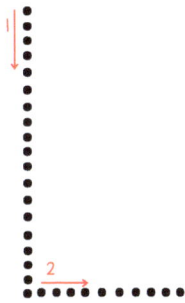

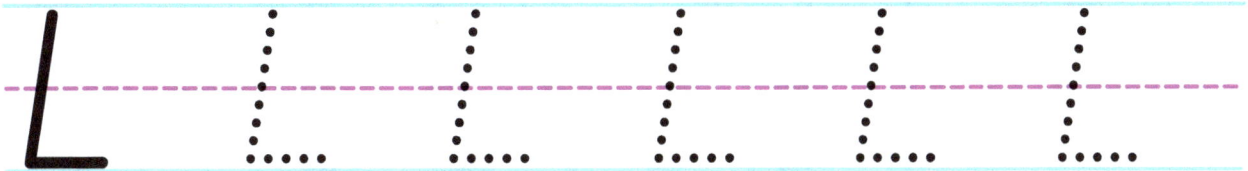

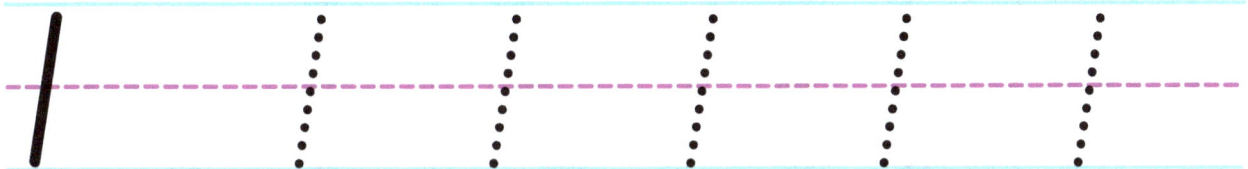

DIRECTIONS: PRACTICE TRACING AND WRITING EACH LETTER IN THE SPACE PROVIDED.

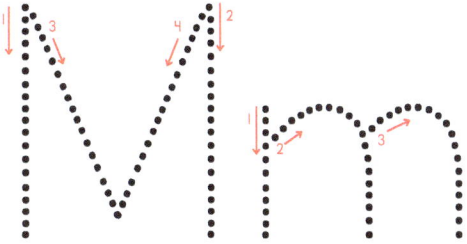

Mm

M M M M M M

M M M M M M

M

M

DIRECTIONS: PRACTICE TRACING AND WRITING EACH LETTER IN THE SPACE PROVIDED.

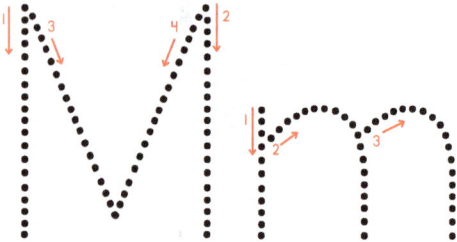

Mm

m
m
m
m

DIRECTIONS: PRACTICE TRACING AND WRITING EACH LETTER IN THE SPACE PROVIDED.

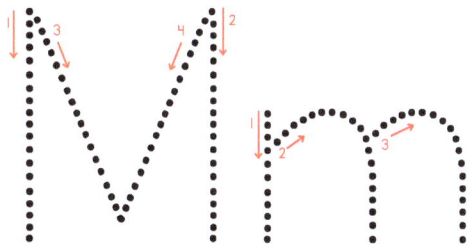

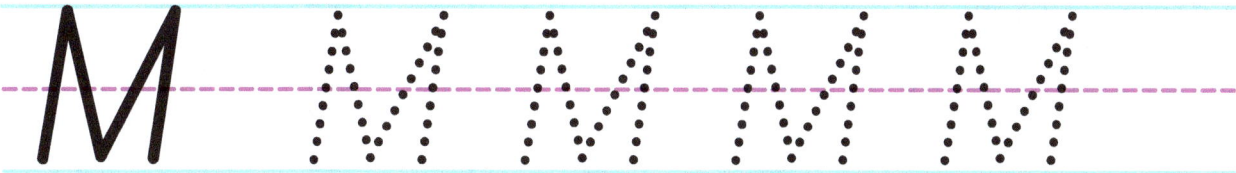

Mm

M   M   M   M   M   M

m   m   m   m   m   m

M

m

N

DIRECTIONS: PRACTICE TRACING AND WRITING EACH LETTER IN THE SPACE PROVIDED.

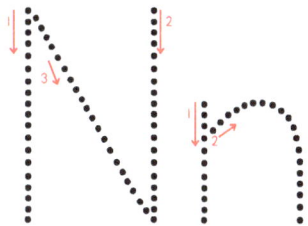

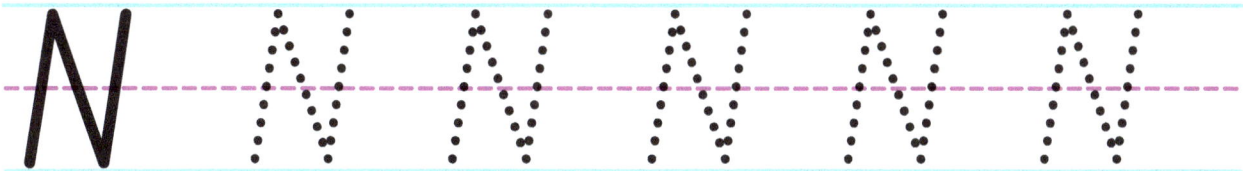

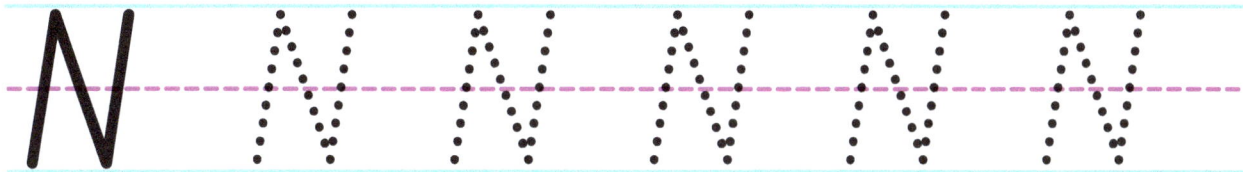

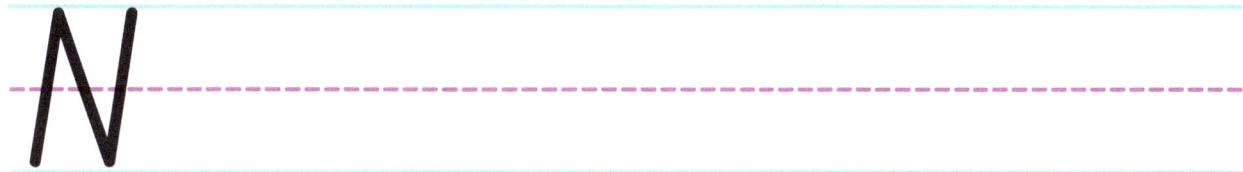

Nn

N N N N N N N N N N N

N N N N N N N N N N N

N

N

DIRECTIONS: PRACTICE TRACING AND WRITING EACH LETTER IN THE SPACE PROVIDED.

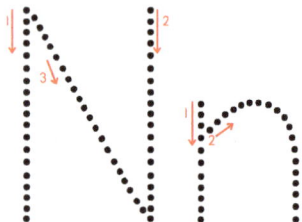

Nn

n   n   n   n   n   n

n   n   n   n   n   n

n

n

DIRECTIONS: PRACTICE TRACING AND WRITING EACH LETTER IN THE SPACE PROVIDED.

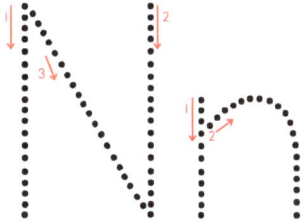

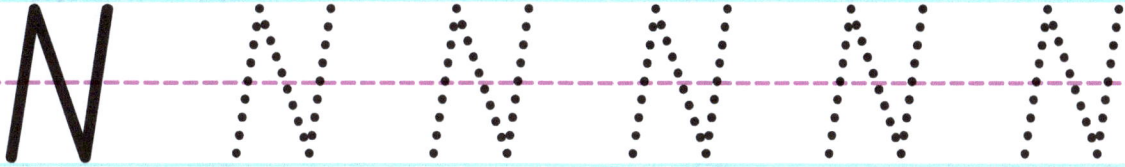

N n

N N N N N N

n n n n n n

N

n

O

DIRECTIONS: PRACTICE TRACING AND WRITING EACH LETTER IN THE SPACE PROVIDED.

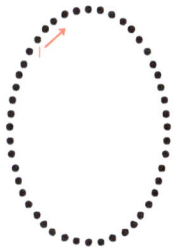

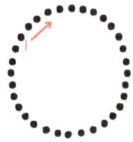

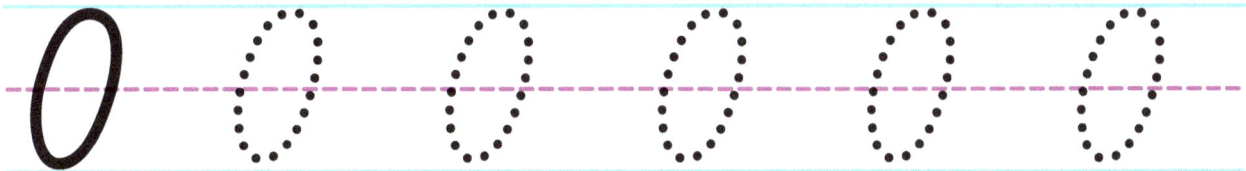

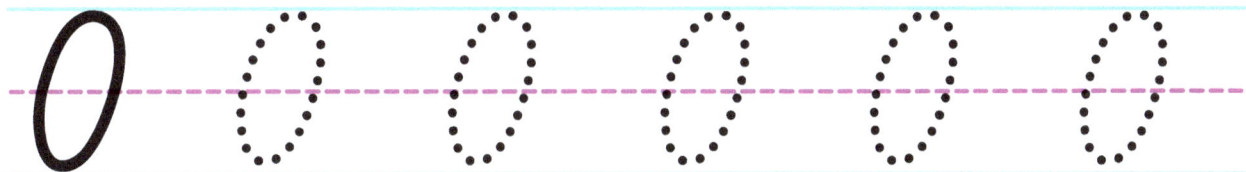

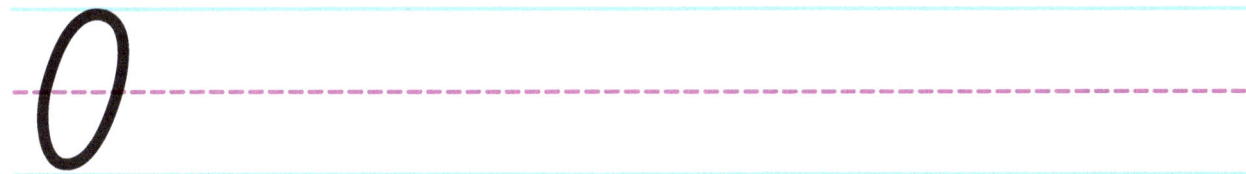

O o

O O O O O O

O O O O O O

O

O

DIRECTIONS: PRACTICE TRACING AND WRITING EACH LETTER IN THE SPACE PROVIDED.

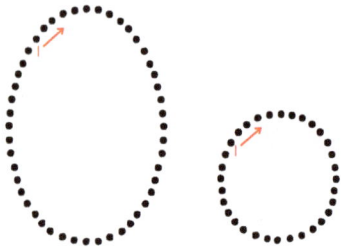

O o

O   o   o   o   o   o

O   o   o   o   o   o

O

O

DIRECTIONS: PRACTICE TRACING AND WRITING EACH LETTER IN THE SPACE PROVIDED.

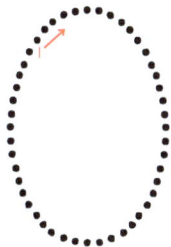

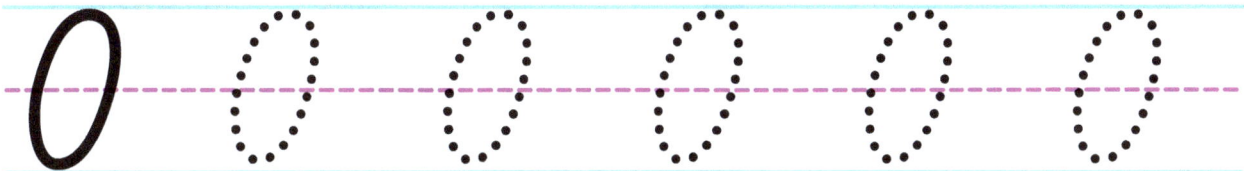

O o

O O O O O O

O O O O O O

O

O

DIRECTIONS: PRACTICE TRACING AND WRITING EACH LETTER IN THE SPACE PROVIDED.

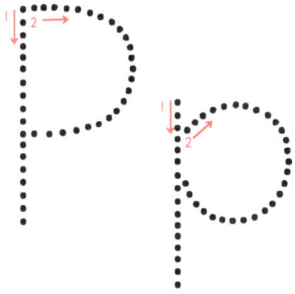

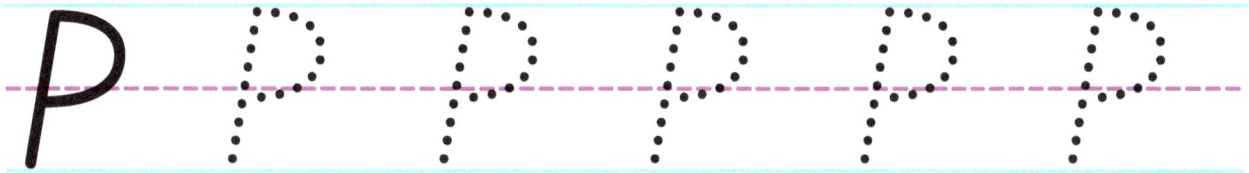

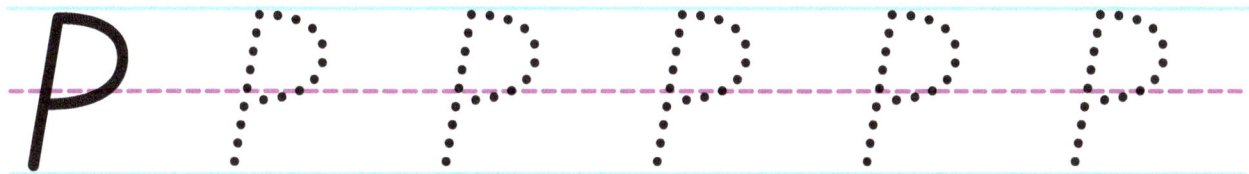

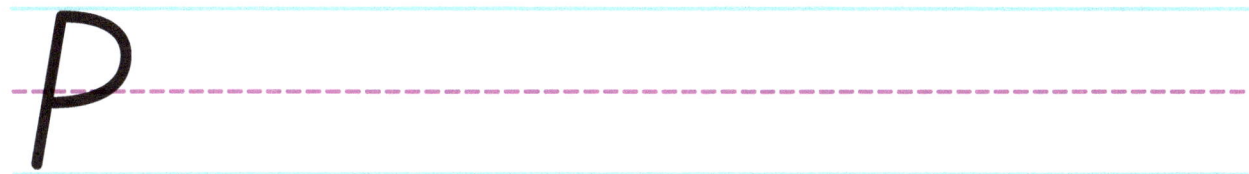

P p

P P P P P P

P P P P P P

P

P

DIRECTIONS: PRACTICE TRACING AND WRITING EACH LETTER IN THE SPACE PROVIDED.

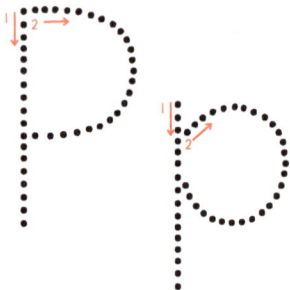

p   p   p   p   p   p   p

p   p   p   p   p   p   p

p

p

DIRECTIONS: PRACTICE TRACING AND WRITING EACH LETTER IN THE SPACE PROVIDED.

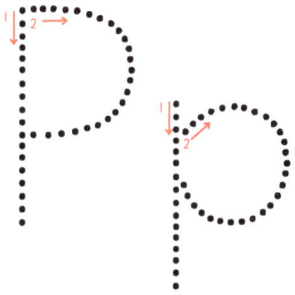

P p

P P P P P P

p p p p p p

P

p

DIRECTIONS: PRACTICE TRACING AND WRITING EACH LETTER IN THE SPACE PROVIDED.

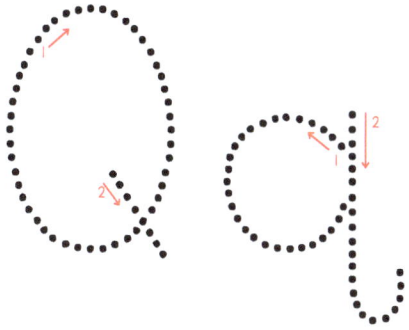

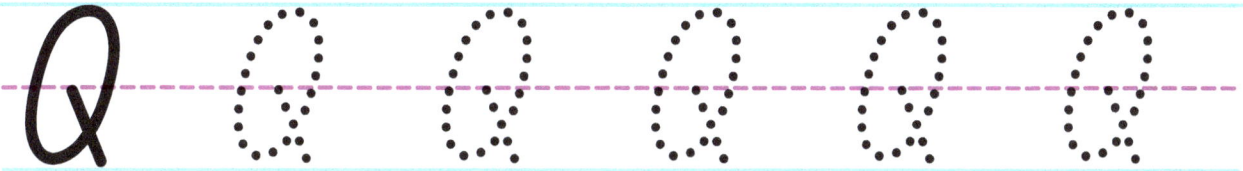

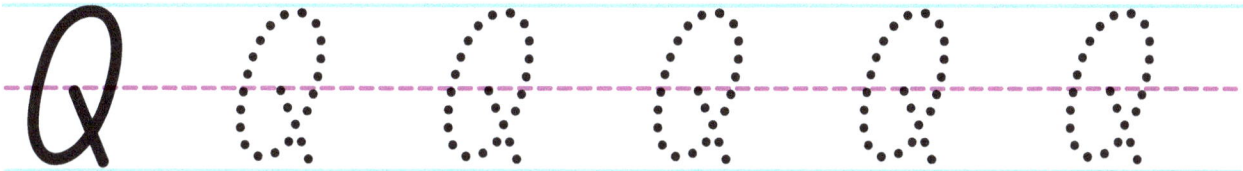

Q q

Q   Q   Q   Q   Q   Q

Q   Q   Q   Q   Q   Q

Q

Q

DIRECTIONS: PRACTICE TRACING AND WRITING EACH LETTER IN THE SPACE PROVIDED.

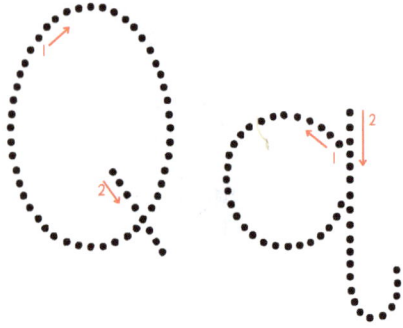

Q q

q   q   q   q   q   q

q   q   q   q   q   q

q

q

DIRECTIONS: PRACTICE TRACING AND WRITING EACH LETTER IN THE SPACE PROVIDED.

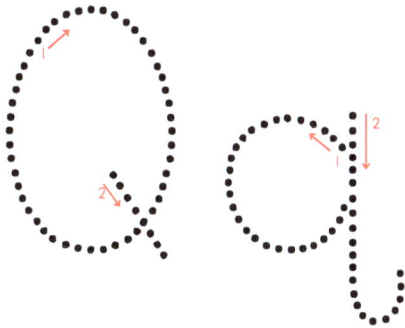

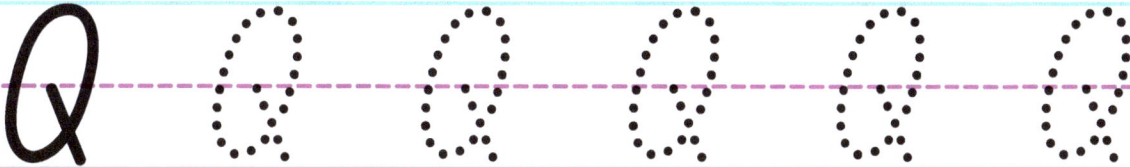

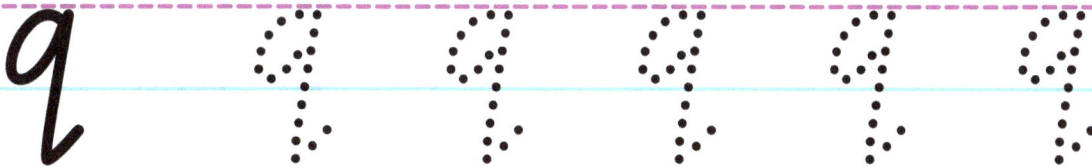

Q q

Q Q Q Q Q Q

q q q q q q

Q

q

DIRECTIONS: PRACTICE TRACING AND WRITING EACH LETTER IN THE SPACE PROVIDED.

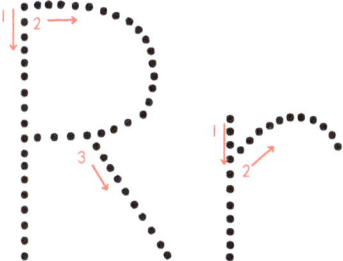

R r

R R R R R R

R R R R R R

R

R

DIRECTIONS: PRACTICE TRACING AND WRITING EACH LETTER IN THE SPACE PROVIDED.

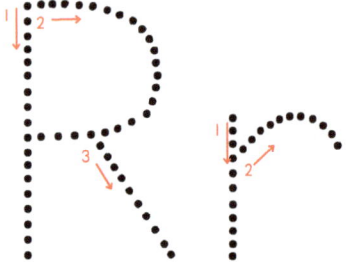

Rr

r   r   r   r   r   r

r   r   r   r   r   r

r

r

DIRECTIONS: PRACTICE TRACING AND WRITING EACH LETTER IN THE SPACE PROVIDED.

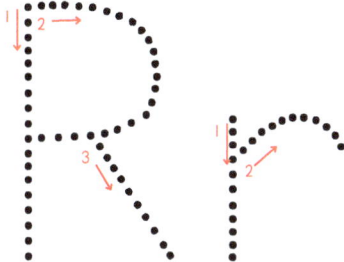

R r

R R R R R R

r r r r r r

R

r

DIRECTIONS: PRACTICE TRACING AND WRITING EACH LETTER IN THE SPACE PROVIDED.

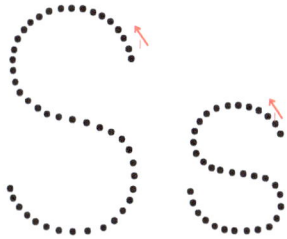

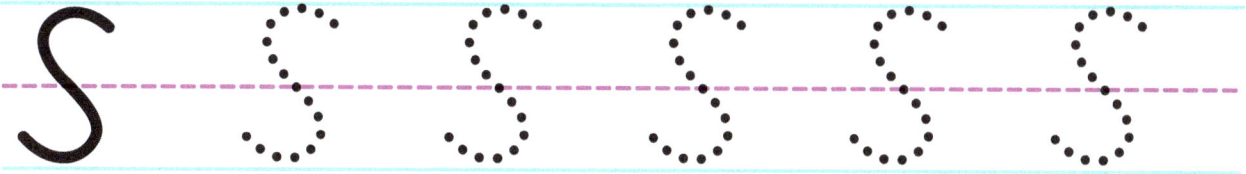

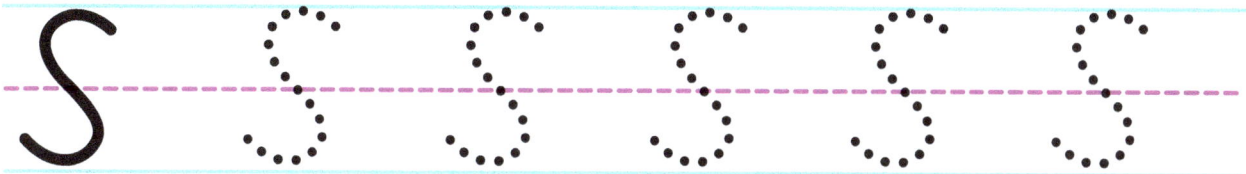

S s

S S S S S S

S S S S S S

S

S

DIRECTIONS: PRACTICE TRACING AND WRITING EACH LETTER IN THE SPACE PROVIDED.

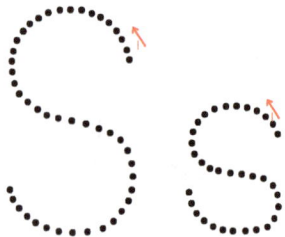

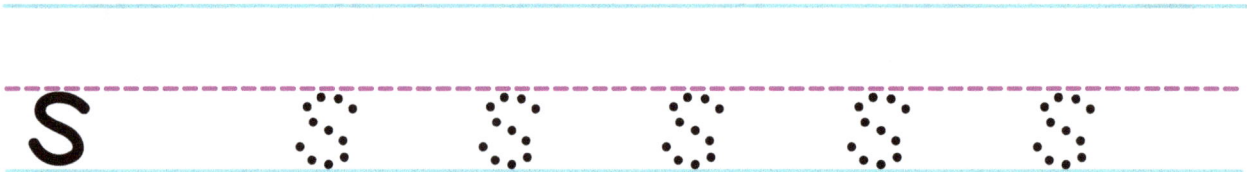

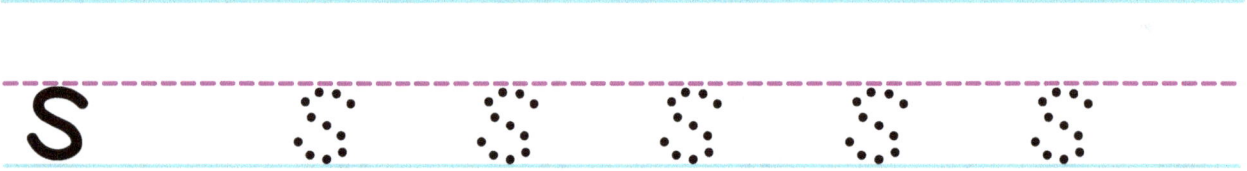

S s

S S S S S S

s s s s s s

S

s

DIRECTIONS: PRACTICE TRACING AND WRITING EACH LETTER IN THE SPACE PROVIDED.

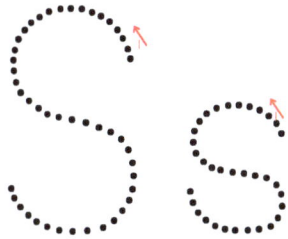

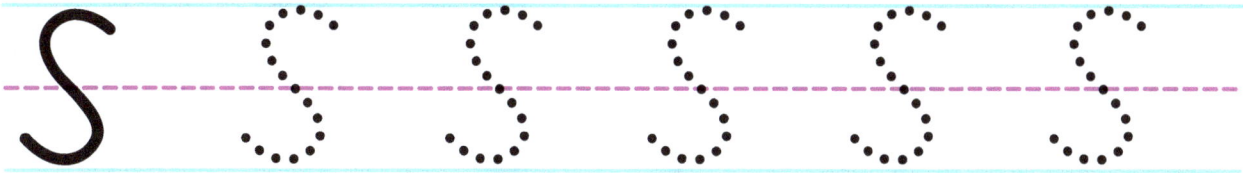

S s

S S S S S S

s s s s s s

S

s

DIRECTIONS: PRACTICE TRACING AND WRITING EACH LETTER IN THE SPACE PROVIDED.

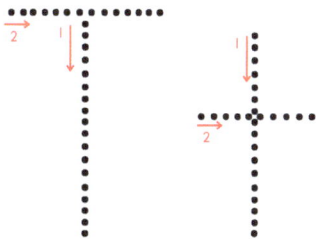

T   t

T   T   T   T   T

T   T   T   T   T

T

T

DIRECTIONS: PRACTICE TRACING AND WRITING EACH LETTER IN THE SPACE PROVIDED.

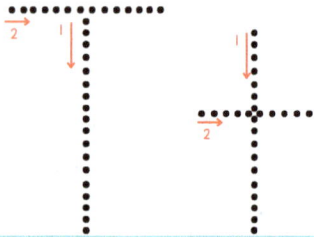

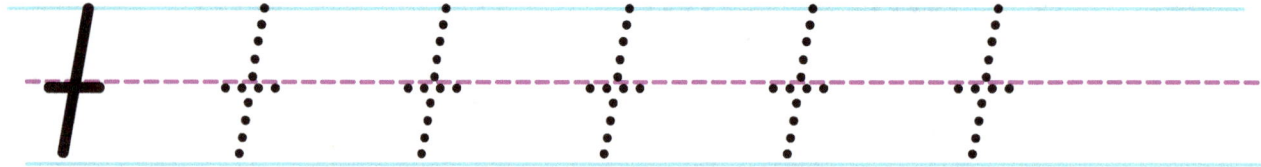

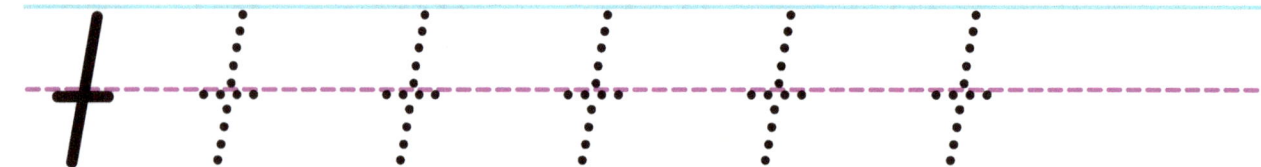

DIRECTIONS: PRACTICE TRACING AND WRITING EACH LETTER IN THE SPACE PROVIDED.

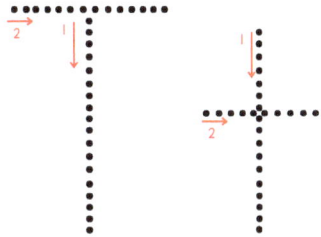

DIRECTIONS: PRACTICE TRACING AND WRITING EACH LETTER IN THE SPACE PROVIDED.

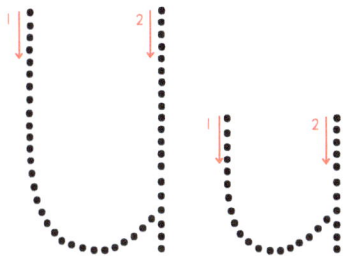

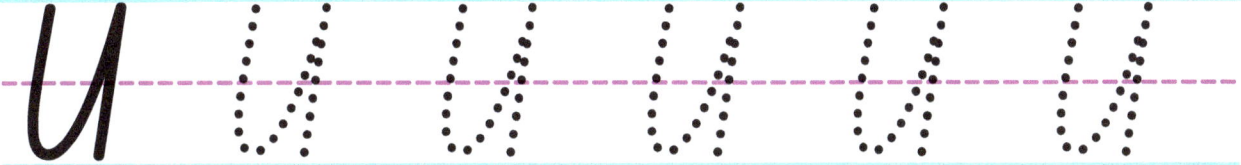

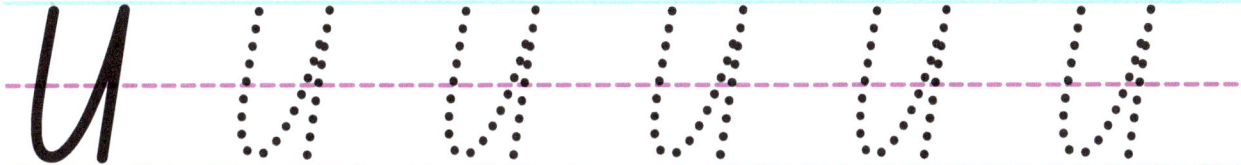

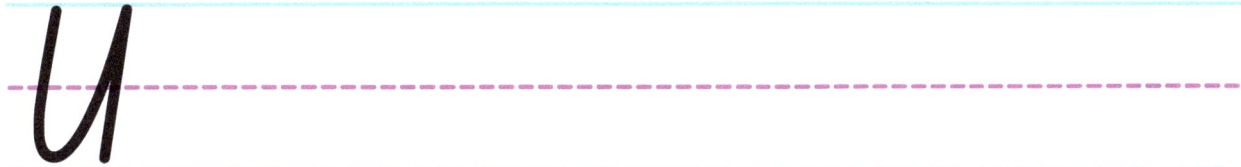

U u

U U U U U U

U U U U U U

U

U

DIRECTIONS: PRACTICE TRACING AND WRITING EACH LETTER IN THE SPACE PROVIDED.

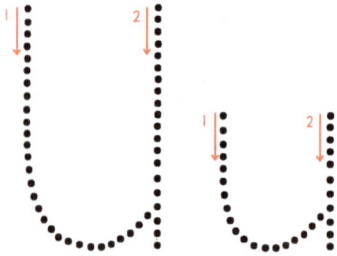

U u

u u u u u u

U U U U U U

u

u

DIRECTIONS: PRACTICE TRACING AND WRITING EACH LETTER IN THE SPACE PROVIDED.

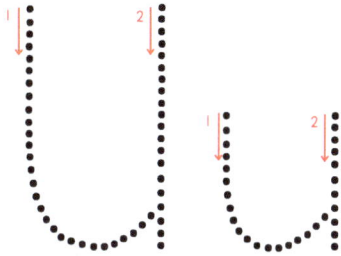

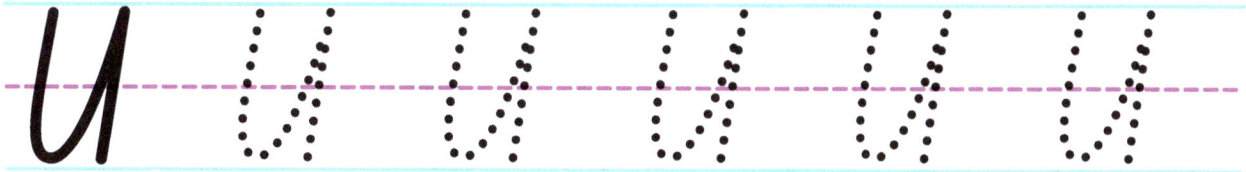

U u

U U U U U U

u u u u u u

U

u

DIRECTIONS: PRACTICE TRACING AND WRITING EACH LETTER IN THE SPACE PROVIDED.

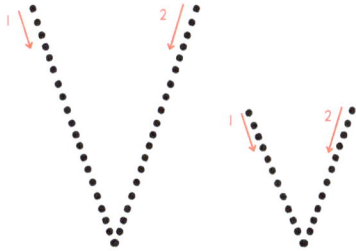

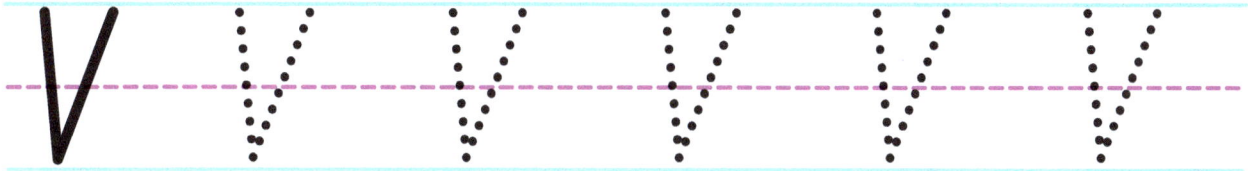

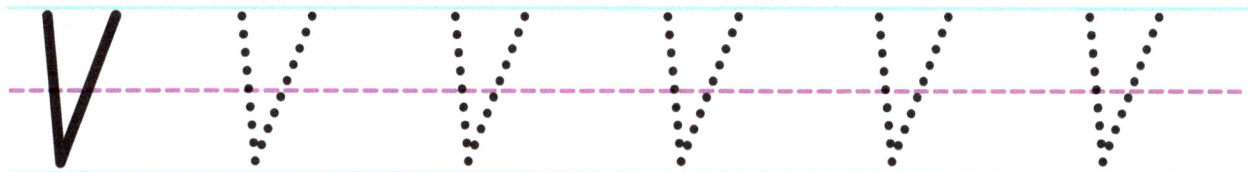

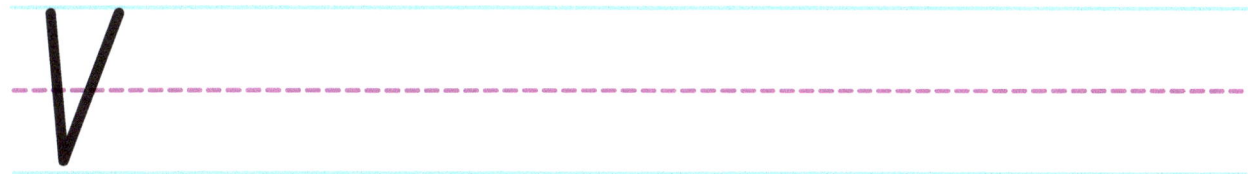

DIRECTIONS: PRACTICE TRACING AND WRITING EACH LETTER IN THE SPACE PROVIDED.

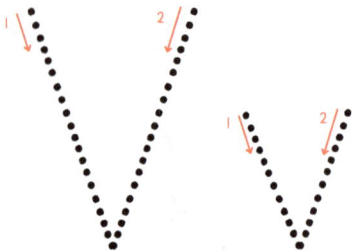

V v

v   v   v   v   v   v

V   V   V   V   V   V

V

V

DIRECTIONS: PRACTICE TRACING AND WRITING EACH LETTER IN THE SPACE PROVIDED.

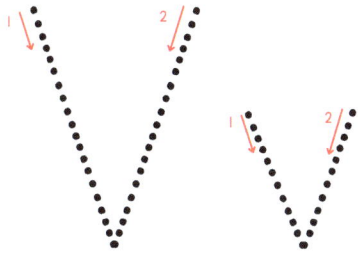

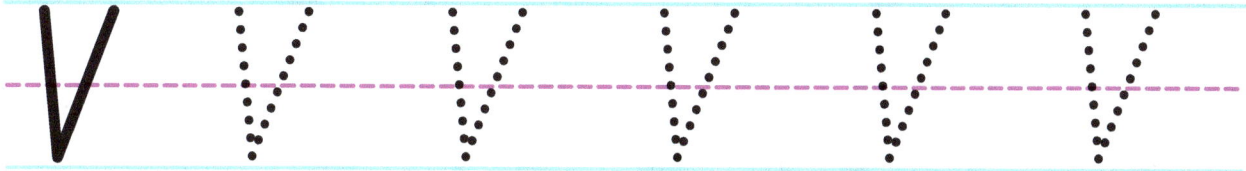

V v

V V V V V V V

v v v v v v

V

v

DIRECTIONS: PRACTICE TRACING AND WRITING EACH LETTER IN THE SPACE PROVIDED.

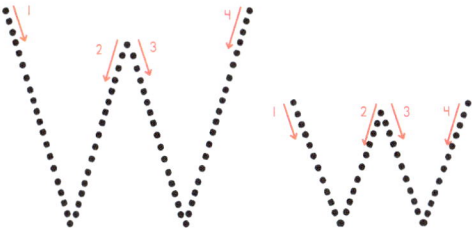

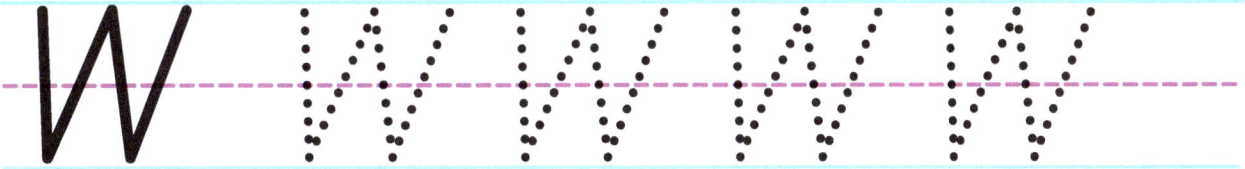

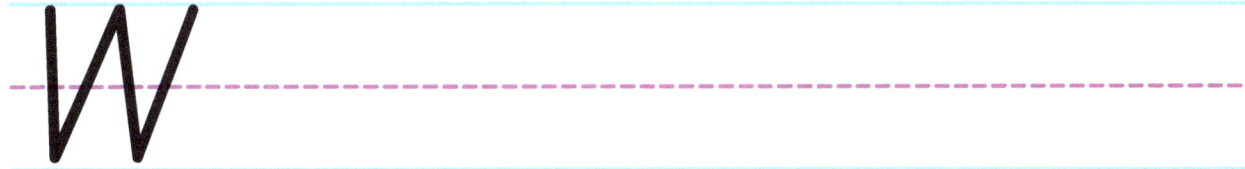

W w

W W W W W W W W W

W W W W W W W W W

W

W

DIRECTIONS: PRACTICE TRACING AND WRITING EACH LETTER IN THE SPACE PROVIDED.

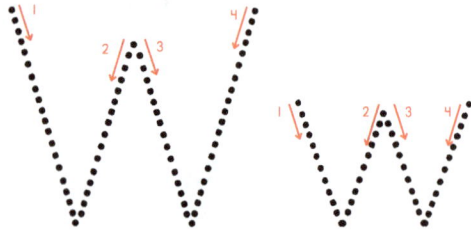

W w

w   w   w   w   w   w

w   w   w   w   w   w

w

w

DIRECTIONS: PRACTICE TRACING AND WRITING EACH LETTER IN THE SPACE PROVIDED.

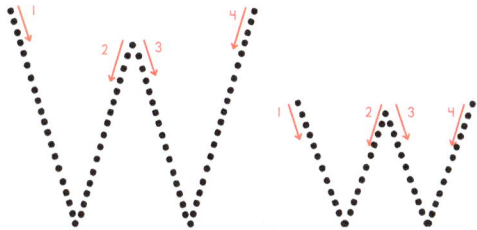

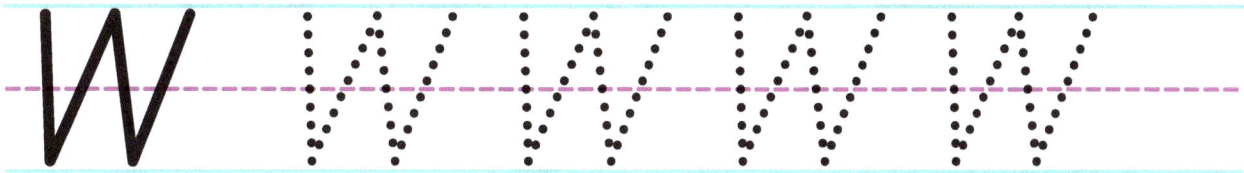

W w

W W W W W W

w w w w w w

W

w

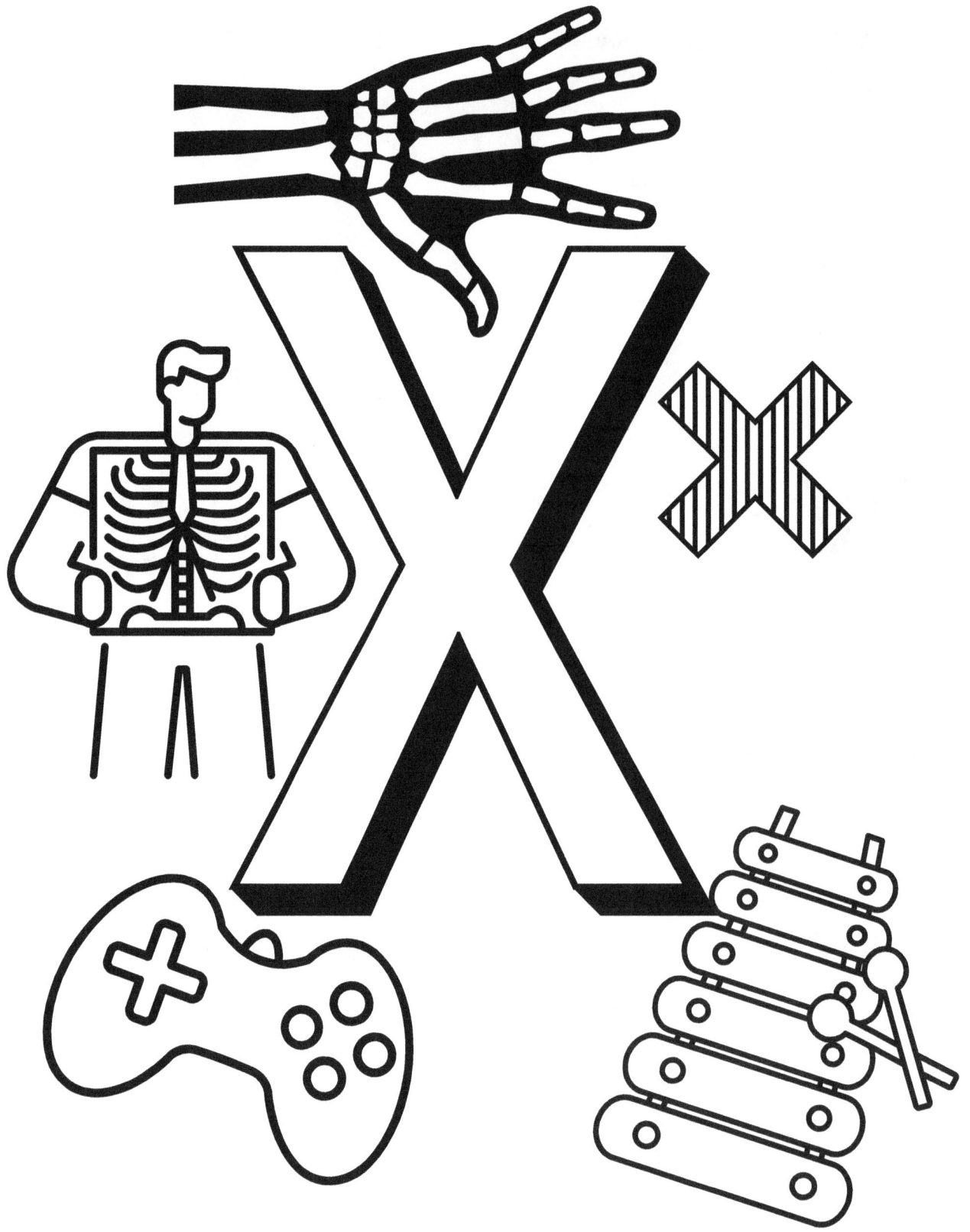

DIRECTIONS: PRACTICE TRACING AND WRITING EACH LETTER IN THE SPACE PROVIDED.

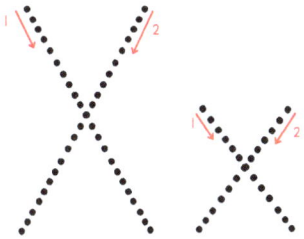

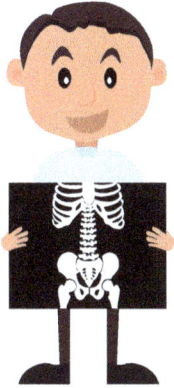

X x

DIRECTIONS: PRACTICE TRACING AND WRITING EACH LETTER IN THE SPACE PROVIDED.

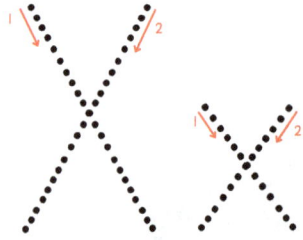

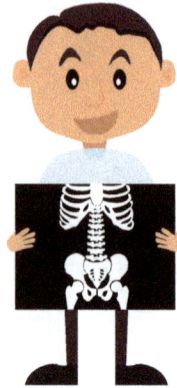

X x

X   X   X   X   X   X

x   x   x   x   x   x

X

x

DIRECTIONS: PRACTICE TRACING AND WRITING EACH LETTER IN THE SPACE PROVIDED.

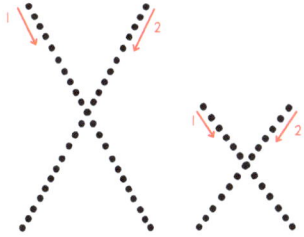

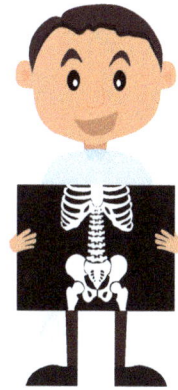

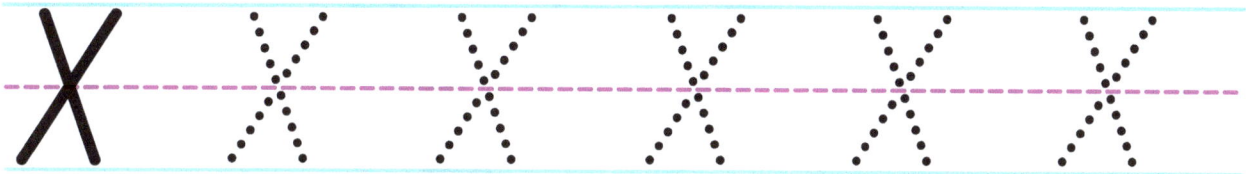

X x

X X X X X X X

X X X X X X

X

X

DIRECTIONS: PRACTICE TRACING AND WRITING EACH LETTER IN THE SPACE PROVIDED.

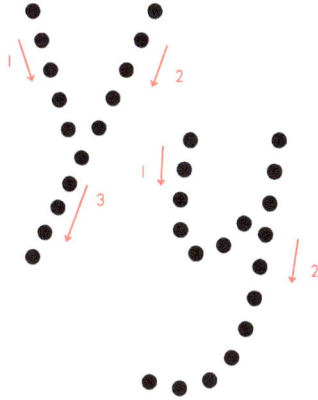

Y y

Y   y   y   y   y   y

Y   y   y   y   y

Y

y

DIRECTIONS: PRACTICE TRACING AND WRITING EACH LETTER IN THE SPACE PROVIDED.

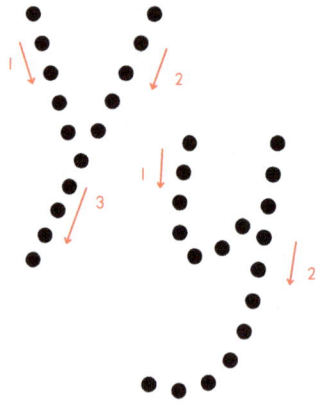

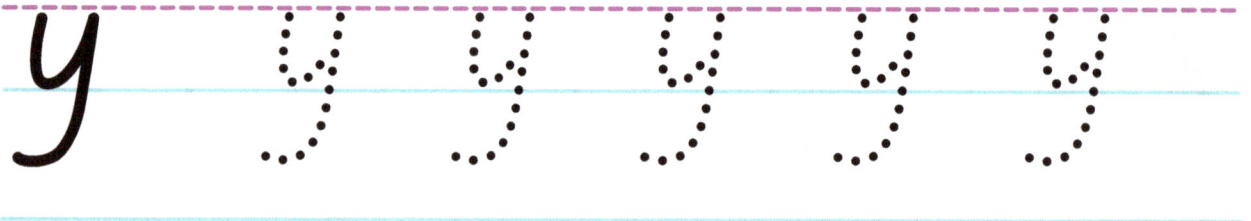

y y y y y y

y y y y y y

y

y

DIRECTIONS: PRACTICE TRACING AND WRITING EACH LETTER IN THE SPACE PROVIDED.

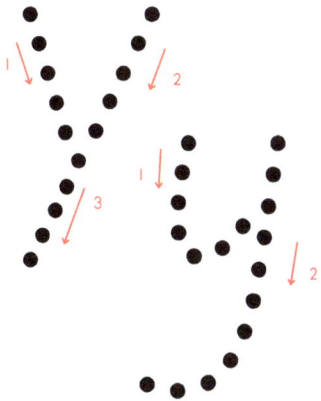

Y y

Y Y Y Y Y Y

y y y y y y

Y

y

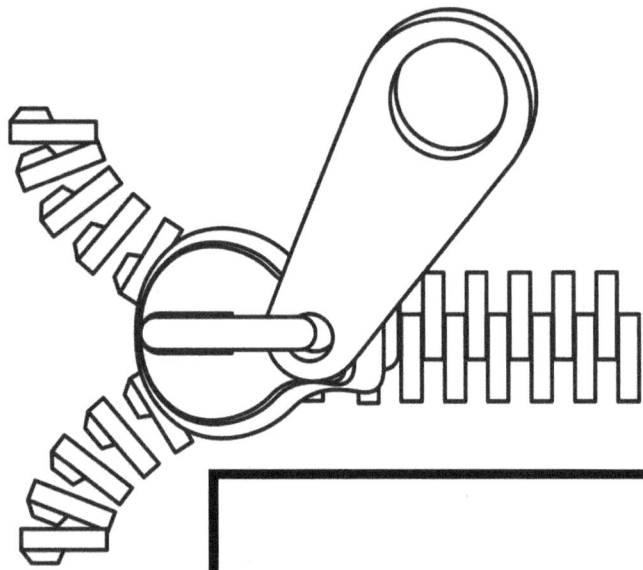

DIRECTIONS: PRACTICE TRACING AND WRITING EACH LETTER IN THE SPACE PROVIDED.

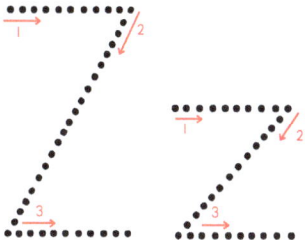

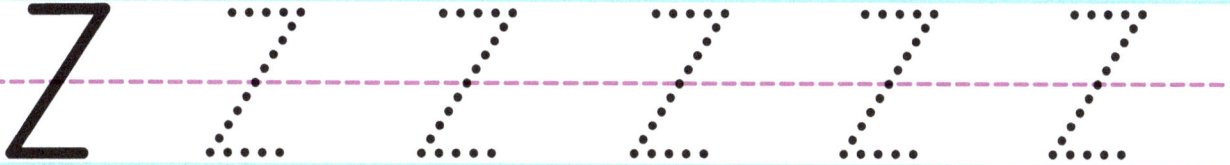

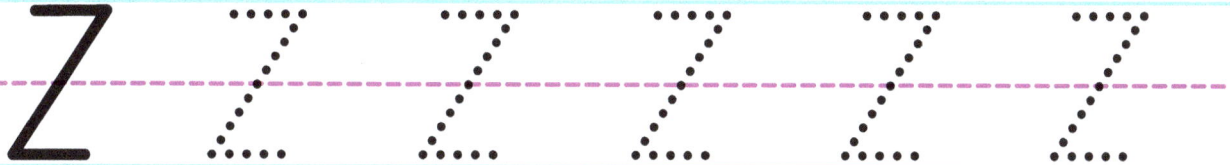

Z z

Z Z Z Z Z Z

Z Z Z Z Z Z

Z

Z

DIRECTIONS: PRACTICE TRACING AND WRITING EACH LETTER IN THE SPACE PROVIDED.

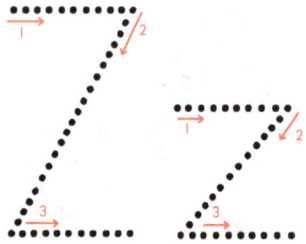

Z z

Z Z Z Z Z Z

Z Z Z Z Z Z

Z

Z

DIRECTIONS: PRACTICE TRACING AND WRITING EACH LETTER IN THE SPACE PROVIDED.

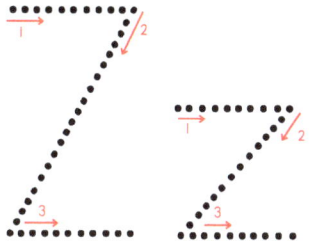

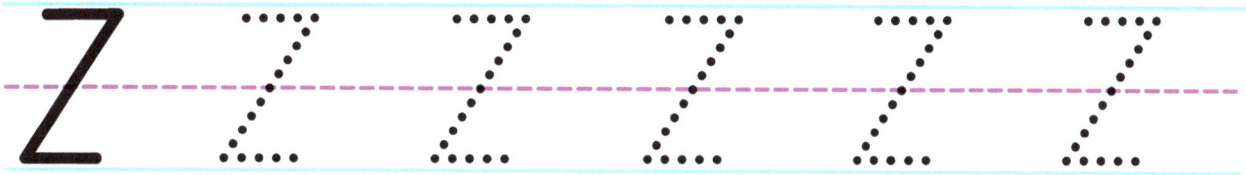

Z z

Z Z Z Z Z Z

z z z z z z

Z

z

Trace the Letters

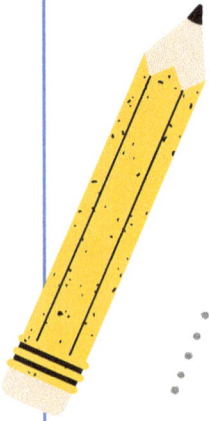

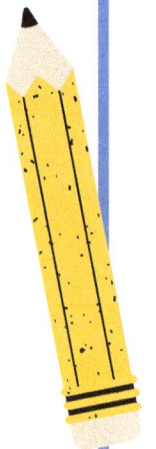

A B C D E

F G H I J K

L M N O P

Q R S T U

V W X Y Z

DIRECTIONS: WRITE THE WORD IN THE SPACE PROVIDED.

I can write

Apple

Apple

Apple

apple

apple

DIRECTIONS: WRITE THE WORD IN THE SPACE PROVIDED.

I can write

Bat

Bat

Bat

bat

bat

DIRECTIONS: WRITE THE WORD IN THE SPACE PROVIDED.

I can write

Cat

Cat

Cat

cat

cat

DIRECTIONS: WRITE THE WORD IN THE SPACE PROVIDED.

I can write

Dog

Dog

Dog

dog

dog

DIRECTIONS: WRITE THE WORD IN THE SPACE PROVIDED.

I can write

Egg

Egg

Egg

egg

egg

DIRECTIONS: WRITE THE WORD IN THE SPACE PROVIDED.

I can write

Fan

Fan

Fan

fan

fan

DIRECTIONS: WRITE THE WORD IN THE SPACE PROVIDED.

I can write

Gift

Gift

Gift

gift

gift

DIRECTIONS: WRITE THE WORD IN THE SPACE PROVIDED.

I can write

Hat

Hat

Hat

hat

hat

DIRECTIONS: WRITE THE WORD IN THE SPACE PROVIDED.

I can write

Igloo

Igloo

Igloo

igloo

igloo

DIRECTIONS: WRITE THE WORD IN THE SPACE PROVIDED.

I can write

Jelly

Jelly

Jelly

jelly

jelly

DIRECTIONS: WRITE THE WORD IN THE SPACE PROVIDED.

I can write

Kite

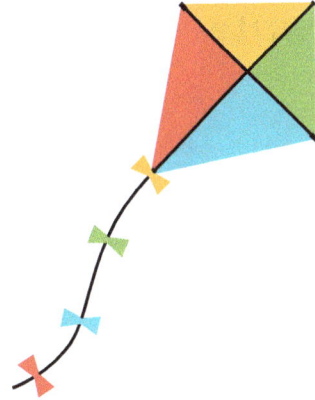

Kite

Kite

kite

kite

DIRECTIONS: WRITE THE WORD IN THE SPACE PROVIDED.

I can write

Lion

Lion

Lion

lion

lion

DIRECTIONS: WRITE THE WORD IN THE SPACE PROVIDED.

I can write

Moon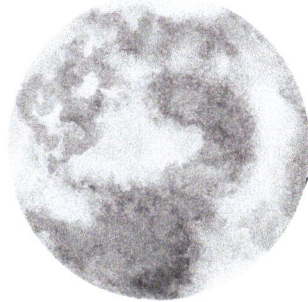

Moon

Moon

moon

moon

DIRECTIONS: WRITE THE WORD IN THE SPACE PROVIDED.

I can write

Net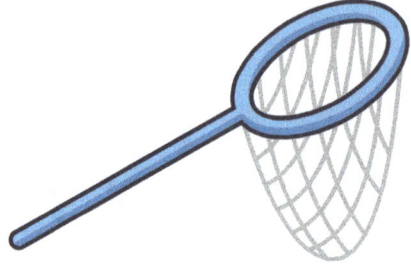

Net

Net

net

net

DIRECTIONS: WRITE THE WORD IN THE SPACE PROVIDED.

I can write

Orange

Orange

Orange

orange

orange

DIRECTIONS: WRITE THE WORD IN THE SPACE PROVIDED.

I can write

Pan

Pan

Pan

pan

pan

DIRECTIONS: WRITE THE WORD IN THE SPACE PROVIDED.

I can write

Queen

Queen

Queen

queen

queen

DIRECTIONS: WRITE THE WORD IN THE SPACE PROVIDED.

I can write

Rabbit

Rabbit

Rabbit

rabbit

rabbit

NAME	DATE

DIRECTIONS: WRITE THE WORD IN THE SPACE PROVIDED.

I can write

Sun

Sun

Sun

sun

sun

DIRECTIONS: WRITE THE WORD IN THE SPACE PROVIDED.

I can write

Tub

Tub

Tub

tub

tub

DIRECTIONS: WRITE THE WORD IN THE SPACE PROVIDED.

I can write

Umbrella

Umbrella

Umbrella

umbrella

umbrella

DIRECTIONS: WRITE THE WORD IN THE SPACE PROVIDED.

I can write

Van

Van

Van

van

van

DIRECTIONS: WRITE THE WORD IN THE SPACE PROVIDED.

I can write

Water

Water

Water

water

water

DIRECTIONS: WRITE THE WORD IN THE SPACE PROVIDED.

I can write

X-ray

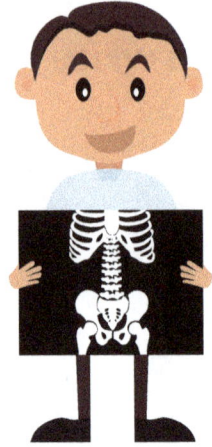

X-ray

X-ray

x-ray

x-ray

DIRECTIONS: WRITE THE WORD IN THE SPACE PROVIDED.

I can write

Yarn

Yarn

Yarn

yarn

yarn

NAME	DATE

DIRECTIONS: WRITE THE WORD IN THE SPACE PROVIDED.

I can write

Zipper

Zipper

Zipper

zipper

zipper

Name: _____

COLOR THE WORD

Color the word that is depicted in the picture.

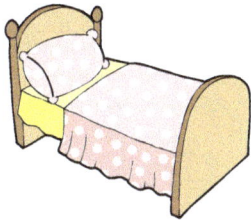

bed	bud

cup	cap

pat	pot

bug	bag

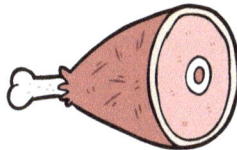

ham	him

cop	cap

tin	ten

fix	fox

six	sax